D0460216

The Gospel in a Pagan Society

Kenneth F. W. Prior

a book for modern evangelists

InterVarsity Press
Downers Grove
Illinois 60515

InterVarsity Press is the book
publishing division of
Inter-Varsity Christian Fellowship,
a student movement active on campus
at hundreds of universities,
colleges and schools of nursing.
For information about local and
regional activities, write
IVCF, 233 Langdon St.,
Madison, WI 53703.

ISBN 0-87784-484-4
Library of Congress Catalog
Card Number: 75-7248

Printed in the United States
of America

Contents

Preface

First a question to preachers (or any other kind of public speaker for that matter): have you ever given an address at five minutes' notice, using someone else's sermon notes? I have, and it was to such an experience that this book owes its origin.

It happened at a convention a few years ago. I had been invited to speak to a meeting of local ministers on Paul's address in Athens, recorded in Acts 17, and usually known as the Areopagus address. Somehow I never got round to preparation before setting out for the convention, so I took with me a couple of commentaries on the Acts and the notes of sermons I had preached at various times on odd verses in the passage in question. The day before the ministers' meeting I was just about to begin my belated preparation, when a telephone call informed me that a group of clergy and ministers in a nearby hall were patiently awaiting the arrival of both chairman and speaker! How the confusion about the actual date of the gathering arose I shall never know. All that mattered for me was that when I rose to speak the brief car ride was all the time for preparation I had had.

I quite expected when I started, to dry up in about five minutes. But as I stood there, with only my Bible in front of me (it is true that I also had with me a bundle of old notes, but on the spur of the moment I could make neither head nor tail of them), my mind seemed to fill with significant ideas from Luke's account of Paul's address, and these together with memories of my previous notes kept me going for quite a while. It was the remark of the chairman as we left the meeting, who I will now reveal was the Reverend Alec Motyer, which really impressed me: 'You ought to write a book on the Areopagus address!' At the time I had not the slightest intention of doing

7

any such thing. Since then he has repeated this suggestion on more than one occasion, and at the same time I have had opportunity for more careful study of this theme in preparing Bible Readings on it for conferences of the Theological Students' Fellowship and ministers of the Evangelical Alliance, and also a series for my own congregation at Sevenoaks Parish Church. So when Mr Edward England of Hodder and Stoughton invited me to write a book on some aspect of evangelism, I decided to offer what follows.

I have for a long time assumed that what we have in Acts 17 is not a complete transcript of all that Paul said, but consists of the notes which Luke took down, or with which Paul later supplied him. If you read the Areopagus address aloud you will find that at the most it takes two minutes, and even to stretch it out to this time you will have to read fairly slowly. Now no one will ever convince me that the great Apostle ever gave an address which lasted only two minutes! So as I spoke at the ministers' meeting, with nothing more than my Bible open in front of me, I was, in effect, speaking from someone else's notes. They consist not only of the main outline of what Paul said, but are expressed presumably in some of the striking phrases which impressed themselves on Luke's mind. And what suggestive points they are! Subsequent study has convinced me that Paul's whole approach demands careful consideration from all who are concerned with communicating the Gospel today.

As Western society departs further from its Christian heritage, and becomes increasingly pagan, we are faced with more and more people who do not share our Christian presuppositions. How are we to make the Gospel meaningful to them and convince them of its truth? Many books have been written which purport to analyse the situation, and new methods are constantly being sought to present the Gospel.

One thing we must never forget is that the pagan situation which now confronts the church is no new one. Not only is it essentially what every pioneer missionary has had to face, but it is the kind of setting in which the Gospel first spread across the world in New Testament times. It is of utmost importance then, that in our discussions about the presentation of the Gospel today, we take into account the manner in which the Apostle to the Gentiles set about preaching the Gospel to the pagan society of his day, and do not waste any of the valuable lessons he left on record.

My study of the Areopagus address has convinced me that this is where Paul has most to teach us on this topic. Luke's account gives us a very clear idea of his approach, his main emphases, the conclusions he drew and the applications he made. I am not going to suggest that Paul's world was in every way that matters identical with ours, nor that the way of success is a slavish following of him in every detail. There are important differences which will emerge in the course of our study. But we can learn valuable lessons from these also, if the way in which Paul adapted himself and applied his message to the people of his day, helps us to do the same for the people of ours.

There has been the suggestion that Paul's policy in Athens was mistaken and that he himself had later misgivings. This is a point of view which, though understandable, I cannot accept, but we shall not be in a position to consider it before the end of the book, when we have completed our examination of Paul's work. We shall not be confining ourselves to the Areopagus address itself, but will look first at the account given in the preceding verses of Paul's witness in Athens over several days. Some misunderstandings of the Areopagus address arise out of a failure to realise that it is Paul's own explanation of the significance of what he had been speaking about in the market place, for the benefit of those who questioned him.

I should like to record my gratitude for help received from three theological college principals! The Reverend Alec Motyer of Trinity College, Bristol, who, in addition to first encouraging me to put pen to paper read my manuscript and offered a number of valuable suggestions. Canon Michael Green, who was then at St John's College, Nottingham and Dr

Raymond Brown of Spurgeon's College filled me in on the subsequent history of the church in Athens, which I thought I ought to know something about, and which proved useful in chapter 12. I have not, however, written just with theological colleges in mind, but hope that the Christian in the pew will feel that what I have written concerns him. So I also owe a debt of thanks to Albert and May Dobson, the verger and his wife at Sevenoaks Parish Church and my highly esteemed fellow workers, for checking that my English is intelligible!

Sowing or Reaping?

A well-known evangelist's efforts in a particular place have been described as 'having apparently made little impression'. Admittedly this is part of an amplified version of the original report, but it fairly reflects the results as estimated by the evangelist's own henchman. The evangelist was none other than the Apostle Paul himself, and the description is from J. B. Phillips' expanded version of Luke's account, which is included at the end of *Letters to Young Churches*. As you have probably guessed, the occasion was Paul's visit to Athens to which we are devoting this book.

Although Luke does in fact reveal that 'some men joined him and believed',[1] Paul's experience is far removed from the unmixed success story that some accounts of present-day evangelism turn out to be, with the latest effort portrayed as the greatest yet. A few years ago a review appeared in a Christian periodical of the write-up of a long series of evangelistic meetings without any hint of failure or disappointment. 'Surely,' the reviewer asked, 'there was just one flop?' To be fair, it is possible that there was not, but isn't it a common experience today that we are often reluctant to admit that the results of organised evangelism are sometimes disappointing? And where there are professions of conversion, don't we often have to concede that these are mostly among those with church backgrounds, while few 'real outsiders' are reached?

Now whereas one would rightly hesitate to describe any of the Apostle's efforts as a flop, a study of the New Testament records of his evangelistic exploits shows that the way was often hard and progress slow. There were times when Paul, human as he was, needed to be encouraged and helped out of a feeling of failure and disappointment.[2] Many of the churches immediately resulting from his preaching were not all that large, even by today's often depressing standards. Yet it was from these small beginnings that the Church of Jesus Christ took root and grew.

All this is very different from the picture that some have of the New Testament situation. It is sometimes assumed that with the experience of Pentecost still fresh, the first Christians were able with the power of the Holy Spirit to carry all before them, with a constant torrent of new converts pouring into the church. If only we could in some way have a repetition of the experience of Pentecost, so it is said, the same results would attend our evangelistic efforts.

Now the last thing we want to do is to detract in any way from what God did on the Day of Pentecost. Nor do we want to discourage any Christian from ensuring that he should not fall short of what God has made available to him through the operation of his Spirit. At the same time however, we must not imagine that in New Testament times success to the extent that they knew it at Pentecost and in the days immediately following, attended their preaching all the time. Later, when we leave Jerusalem and its surroundings, and watch Paul on his missionary journeys, the picture is somewhat different.

Why should this be? Was it that Paul's experience of the Holy Spirit fell short of those who had laboured with such success in Jerusalem? This is the explanation that is sometimes advanced for lack of success in evangelism today. I should like to have heard Paul's answer if this explanation were applied to him!

The answer is surely that evangelism can be one of two forms. All true evangelism would be covered by what has become the standard definition:

To evangelise is so to present Christ Jesus in the power of

the Holy Spirit, that men shall come to put their trust in God
through him, to accept him as their Saviour, and serve him as
their King in the fellowship of his Church.[3]

When, however, we come to describe the actual work of evangelism, or the distinctive task of someone specially called to be
an evangelist, it is defined in two different ways. Some liken it
to sowing, while others conceive of it as reaping. Failure to
recognise these two alternative definitions can cause confusion,
and can lead to people talking at cross purposes. We begin with
the second of them — reaping.

Some years ago I attended a very helpful conference on
evangelism. One of its purposes was to promote understanding
between those engaged in full time itinerant evangelism, and
other ministers including pastors of local churches. I well remember a contribution of a full-time evangelist, who had also
spent some years in pastoral ministry, speaking about the relationship between his work and that of the pastor. He likened
himself to a reaper. The pastor, he explained, sowed the seed,
usually over a relatively long period of time. Then at the op-
portune moment it is the turn of the evangelist to be called in
and reap what has been sown. In this way the faithful work of
the pastor finds fruition, and so the two kinds of ministry are
complementary to each other. He went on to offer another
metaphor likening the evangelist to a midwife. After a period
of gestation he is sent for and the converts are brought to the
birth. The essential gift of the evangelist in this sense is his
ability to 'bring people to decision'. This has often involved the
use of certain techniques (pardon the word) such as inviting
new converts to stand up or 'come forward' as an outward
declaration of their decision.

It is necessary to recognise the assumption underlying this
conception of the work of an evangelist. It is that the potential
convert already has some kind of Christian background as a
result of the pastor's work to which the evangelist can appeal. If
he views his ministry solely in this way, he will not be surprised

if most of his converts have church connections. How can it be otherwise if he is simply reaping where others have sown? Even if the church connections are not too strong, there has still been some previous sowing arising from the surrounding society which in the past has been based on Christian principles. There may, for example, have been a Sunday School background in childhood, or some kind of Christian teaching in day school. At least this is likely to be the case in many countries in the British Commonwealth and the United States.

There has undoubtedly been much successful evangelism of this kind over the past hundred years or so. It has ensured that within a Christian tradition there have been those with a real commitment to Christ. Sankey and Moody and their successors have been very effective in this type of evangelism. Evangelism in British universities has in past years owed a great deal to Christian principles previously learned in public schools and their daily worship in the school chapel. I had experience of this during twelve years of continuing evangelism in a London church. Among the many who professed conversion at guest services and other evangelistic gatherings the majority had some kind of Christian background whether through church, home or school. Many of them would have called themselves Christians, even though they had never understood what commitment to Christ really meant. It was often something of a shock when they encountered evangelical Christianity either through preaching or in the lives and witness of their Christian friends, and they discovered that for all their respectability they were not real Christians in the New Testament sense after all. So their account of their conversion would often run like this: 'I thought I was a Christian until I met . . .' For such people all they needed in many cases was simply to be told what a real Christian is, without any need to argue that Christianity is true.

No Christian who has been brought up in the circumstances we have described can deny that such evangelism has been, and in some form will continue to be necessary. Whenever there is an existing church, there are likely to be some whose Christianity is merely nominal, even though it may involve regular church attendance. There are also many on the fringe of membership, who make occasional attendances at major festivals, bring their children for baptism and expect to be finally 'brought into church', even though it will involve being carried feet first!

Now all this is the type of evangelism which we read of in the early chapters of Acts. Take what happened on the Day of Pentecost. The many who heard the Apostles and from whom the three thousand converts were drawn, were certainly not complete pagans. Many of them were Jews who lived in Jerusalem and its immediate vicinity. They had spent all their lives in the proximity of the Temple with all that it taught and stood for. Others were Jews of the Dispersion who lived in other parts of the world, but who cared enough to come up to Jerusalem for the feast of Pentecost. A third group represented were not Jews by race, but Gentiles who had been convinced of the value of the Jewish religion, in many cases through the enthusiastic proselytising activity of the Jews, and had come to embrace it for themselves. The people in Jerusalem that day, as Luke summarises it, included, 'both Jews and proselytes, Cretans and Arabians'.[4]

What all these people held in common was their Old Testament background, with its high moral principles such as the Ten Commandments, expectations of a coming Messiah and, above all, lofty conception of the being and character of God. This clearly affected Peter's approach to them, evidenced as it is by his quotations from the Prophet Joel and the Psalms. In particular, he assumed that when he claimed that God had made Jesus 'both Lord and Christ',[5] they would know what he was talking about.

The results of evangelism on ground prepared by Old Testament teaching were impressive. The small handful of disciples that emerged from the upper room on the Day of Pentecost found themselves suddenly augmented by the addition of 'about three thousand souls'.[6] During the days that followed church expansion continued as 'the Lord added to their number day by day those who were being saved'.[7] Two chapters later Luke records a further five thousand who believed on hearing the word.[8] Chapter six opens with the disciples still 'increasing in number', and then summarises progress:

> The word of God increased; and the number of the disciples multiplied greatly in Jerusalem, and a great many of the priests were obedient to the faith.[9]

Note however that all this was *in Jerusalem* where for centuries prophet and priest had sown God's truth, and where the New Testament preachers were now reaping with such outstanding effectiveness. Is this quite the same as evangelising those with a Christian background? Perhaps not entirely, although the kind of basic attitude maintained by a first century Jew is by no means dissimilar to the respectability of many a nominal Christian today. There are however examples of evangelism within the churches of the New Testament, which often seemed, judging from Paul's letters to them, to be as much a mixture of real and nominal Christianity as we find in the churches of today. Was it not to people Paul addressed as 'the church of God which is at Corinth' to whom he appealed 'be reconciled to God'?[10] So we shall continue to proclaim the Gospel in our churches while there are professing Christians who lack a living experience of Christ. As long as there are others around us, who have some recognition of Christian standards in matters of morality, and who in some sense acknowledge the church, we shall invite them to our guest services and other means which are specially geared to reach them.

And now what about those with no Christian background, and who share few, if any of our presuppositions? There are an increasing number of these around us, and the reaching of them is the chief topic of this book. They may still attend church for the occasional funeral or wedding, because they have friends who think like that, but at no other times, not even Christmas or Easter. The previous generation excused their lack of church attendance because they did their bit when they were children, when they were forced to attend three times a Sunday. We now have a generation which has grown up without any childhood membership of Sunday School and with an almost complete ignorance of the most basic points of the Christian faith. Although their parents rarely went to church, they still held to Christian morality, and thought that by observing it they had a reasonable chance of heaven when they died. This is no longer the case and Christian moral standards can never be taken for granted. Francis Schaeffer has described this change in society as follows.

In the United States in the short span from the twenties to the sixties we have seen a complete shift. Of course not every one in the United States in the twenties was a Christian, but in general there was a Christian consensus. Now that consensus is completely gone. Ours is a post Christian world in which Christianity, not only in the number of Christians but in cultural emphasis and cultural result, is now in the absolute minority. To ask young people to maintain the status quo is folly. The status quo is no longer ours ... When we begin to think of them and preach the Gospel to them, we must begin with the fact that they have no knowledge of biblical Christianity. But it is more than this, for the whole culture has shifted from Christian to post-Christian.[11]

This is in all essentials the situation faced by the preachers of the Gospel in the first century. Once they travelled outside Palestine, they found themselves among people who were every bit as ignorant of the God revealed in Scripture as many of our contemporaries today. Nobody went to church and there was no Sunday. Morals were as permissive as today. The only exception was to be found in the small Jewish community that existed in many of the cities. Sometimes these were large enough for a synagogue to be formed. Very often, as at Phillipi, only a handful of women would meet to pray.[12]

How can you describe an evangelist in such a situation? As a reaper, reaping where others have sown? On the contrary, the evangelist is now a pioneer, breaking completely fresh ground. And this was Paul's ministry from the moment he said at Antioch in Pisidia, 'we turn to the Gentiles'.[13] It is true that when he arrived in a new city he usually made the synagogue his first point of contact, but he regarded himself first and foremost as 'an Apostle to the Gentiles',[14] and his call to this ministry he traced right back to the beginning of his Christian experience.[15]

This ministry had many differences from that among the Jews and their Gentile proselytes. In particular progress was far slower. Paul had his successes among the Gentiles, it is true. In addition to the Gentiles who attended the synagogues and responded in large numbers when they heard Paul preach there,[16] there was encouragement at Derbe where he and Barnabas 'made many disciples'[17] and at the beginning of the second missionary journey.[18] Yet we cannot fail to notice that there are no examples of converts being numbered in thousands as they had known in Jerusalem and its district at Pentecost and the days immediately following. Sometimes results among complete pagans were quite small, as Paul found at Athens. So we are bound to agree with the observation of Michael Green: 'The Christian faith grew fastest and best on Jewish soil, or at least on soil which had been prepared by Judaism.'[19]

Yet in spite of its difficulties and slowness in showing results, Paul gloried in pioneering evangelism, which involved sowing the seed of the Gospel in virgin soil, and he made it the dominant aim of his life. Here is how he described this ministry:

Making it my ambition to preach the Gospel, not where Christ has already been named, lest I should build on another man's foundation, but as it is written, 'They shall see who have never been told of him, and they shall understand who have never heard of him.'[20]

In another passage he confesses that this is a privilege which leaves him with a sense of complete unworthiness:

> To me, though I am the very least of all the saints, this grace was given, to preach among the Gentiles the unsearchable riches of Christ.[21]

It was such an attitude which enabled Paul to persevere when the task was uphill and discouraging. Even when he was about to explain that his hearers' slowness to recognise the truth of his gospel arose from a spiritual blindness which was satanic in origin, he was still able to write, 'Therefore, having this ministry by the mercy of God, we do not lose heart.'[22]

We have to recognise that this conception of the evangelist as a sower and pioneer rather than a reaper has not been the dominant one since Victorian times. As a recent report on evangelism has put it:

> Over the last one hundred years this function has been increasingly exercised in a way which has emphasised the public rather than the personal, and reaping rather than sowing.[23]

Faced as we are with a pagan society to evangelise, this will do no longer. We need to recapture something of the Apostle's sense of thrill at the prospect of pioneer evangelism. When our society was more Christian than it is today, this was largely reserved for overseas missionaries. Many a Christian at home found the romance of their lives irresistible, even if their response to the missionary call never went beyond the realms of fantasy. How many young Christians, for example, have felt 'called' to China through reading the life of Hudson Taylor! Today we do not have to be surrounded by Chinese pagodas, Hindu temples or Mohammedan mosques to be in a pioneering situation. Right where we are we are among people 'who have never heard of him'. So while we shall not neglect the so-called religious people who need the Gospel ('to the Jew first', as Paul would have put it), an increasing number of us must share his 'ambition to preach the Gospel, not where Christ has already been named'.

Art Forms and Idols

Paul's time in Athens began with a sightseeing tour. There has always been much to see in that city, as is still the case today. So while he was awaiting the arrival of his companions, Silas and Timothy, whom he had left behind in Thessalonica, he decided to take a look round. What he saw affected him deeply.

> Now while Paul was waiting for them in Athens, his spirit was provoked within him as he saw that the city was full of idols.[1]

We know from the ruins still standing today and from exhibits in our museums, that first century Athens abounded in works of art, both architecture and sculpture. What we don't always remember is the religious significance that they held, and that so many of them were, in fact, idols. To New Testament Christians like Paul this mattered much more than any artistic merit they may have possessed. As Professor Blaiklock in his Rendle Short memorial lecture pointed out,

> Those who view with wonder the magnificence of Athens' ruined heart today, are without the Jews' deep loathing of idolatry.[2]

This was the attitude in which Paul had been nurtured. Not only did the Law of God forbid the worship of other gods, as the first of the Ten Commandments made clear, but Jehovah himself was not to be worshipped in an idolatrous fashion either. This was forbidden in the second of the Commandments. What God's Law commanded, the prophets constantly preached to a people that found it all too easy to fall for the temptation to imitate the idolatrous practices of the surrounding tribes. Not that they necessarily worshipped pagan deities as they did in the Northern Kingdom during the reign of Ahab, when his wife Jezebel, a heathen princess, introduced her own native god Baal, together with hundreds of prophets to propagate his religion. Often they compromised the worship of Jehovah with idolatry, when they set up the metal bull at the high places, accompanied by the degrading practices associated with it. So even when the worship of Baal was banned by the better kings, the following proviso had often to be added: 'Yet the high places were not taken away, and the people still sacrificed and burned incense on the high places.'[3]

The time came, however, when the battle against idolatry was decisively won, and the people of God learned once and for all the lesson that generations of prophets had tried to bring home to them. That happened during the exile, and when they returned to their own land, it was as a people purified from the defilement of idolatry. It was just as one of the prophets of the exile said it would be:

> For I will take you from the nations, and gather you from all the countries, and bring you into your own land. I will sprinkle clean water upon you, and you shall be clean from all your uncleannesses, and *from all your idols* I will cleanse you.[4]

The post-exilic Jews certainly had their faults, but idolatry wasn't one of them. They had learnt their lesson the hard way and it would never be forgotten.

This was the attitude inherited by the New Testament Christians from their Jewish predecessors and which they took with them as they evangelised in the Greek cities. It accounts for the way that Paul and Barnabas recoiled in horror when they themselves became the objects of idolatry at Lystra by a crowd that had been carried away with unthinking enthusiasm by the spectacle of Paul healing a cripple. He protested:

> Men, why are you doing this? We also are men of like nature with you, and bring you good news, that you should turn from these vain things to a living God who made the heaven and the earth . . .[5]

When we come to Acts 17 it is perhaps of some significance that Luke uses an Old Testament word to describe Paul's reaction to the idolatry of Athens. The word translated 'provoked' (R.S.V.) and 'stirred' (A.V.) is the one used in the Septuagint[6] of Jehovah being provoked to anger by idolatry.

Turning from idolatry was expected by the Apostles of their converts and was one of the most obvious ways in which someone converted out of paganism would give evidence of his repentance. It was in such terms that Paul reminded the Thessalonians of their conversion: '. . . how you turned to God from idols, to serve a living and true God.'[7]

Why then, did the early Christians make such an uncompromising stand on the question of idolatry? It was certainly not that they disapproved of art. Indeed in the Old Testament a great deal of use had been made of it. No less a person than Moses, who had been given the task of delivering God's commandments, including those concerned with idolatry, was at the same time involved with much art work in the Tabernacle. The curtains, for example, were adorned with embroidered figures, there were the cherubim overshadowing the Ark of the Covenant and the golden candlesticks in the form of a tree. Solomon's Temple, which later replaced the Tabernacle, was no less adorned. We read that Solomon

carved all the wall of the house round about with carved

figures of cherubim and palm trees and open flowers, in the inner and outer rooms.[8]

One of the obvious objections that the Jews would have to the worship of idols is that they were usurping the place that belonged to Jehovah alone. Christians, jealous for the glory of Jesus Christ could not tolerate any rivals either. To them the truth 'Jesus is Lord' lay at the very heart of what they believed and lived for, and was a dignity he could share with no other. So they had to make their position regarding idolatry unmistakably plain. As Michael Green has expressed their point of view,

> It would be pointless to preach Jesus as Lord if he were merely to be thought of as an addition to an already over-crowded pantheon.[9]

Indeed the account of Paul in Athens provides a clear example of this very danger. Whether it was through difficulties of language or dialect it is impossible to tell, but some of Paul's hearers thought he was offering them two extra deities, 'Jesus and the Resurrection'.[10]

One of the chief points the Old Testament makes about idolatry is to draw attention to its futility. All that idolaters succeed in doing is to worship 'the works of their own hands'.[11] In the classical passages on this subject in Isaiah the language becomes quite derisory.[12] Having described the skill and ingenuity with which the craftsman makes his idol, Isaiah states how he 'falls down to it and worships it; he prays to it and says, "Deliver me for thou art my God!" '[13]

A few lines later the voice of God comes in with the salutary reminder: 'Remember these things, O Jacob . . . I formed you, you are my servant.'[14]

What has all this to do with presenting the Gospel today? Before we swallow the assumption that the worship of idols is beneath sophisticated twentieth century minds, we ought to appreciate that idols do not have to be physical objects. It is just as possible to have idols in our minds as we create mental images of the kind of God we like to conceive. This is the very thing that people do when they introduce their idea of God with expressions such as, 'I like to think . . .' It is often used to introduce an easy-going God, whose love is assumed to preclude him from punishing sin. In this way it is possible to invent our own God, who may be far removed from the God who has made himself known through Christ and the Bible.

Sometimes the God we invent fits in with the passing fashions of contemporary thought. This was what lay at the root of idolatry in the Old Testament. It meant that Israel compromised their understanding of God which had been revealed to them with the popular ideas of the surrounding pagan tribes. The danger is just the same with us today. There seem to be grounds for saying that this is what John Robinson was doing in his book *Honest to God.* Anyway this is the assessment of J. I. Packer who entitled his critique of John Robinson's views, 'Keep yourselves from Idols'.

The trouble is that when we invent our own ideas of God, we simply create him in our own image, whereas the truth is the opposite — we have been created in God's image. Because of this the gods and goddesses of ancient Greece and Rome were no more than enlarged human beings. They appointed them as heads of department with gods of love, war, travel and so on. Worse than this, men have even projected on to the gods of their own making their sins. It has been said that if the gods and goddesses of ancient Greece were alive today, most of them would be in prison!

There has, however, been no need for Jewish and Christian people, with God revealed to them through the Bible, to resort to their own imaginings. Nor can he be represented by any physical shape. The God of the Bible asks, 'To whom then will you liken God, or with what likeness compare him?'[15]

Simply to ask such a question excludes the possibility of idolatry. John Eddison has asserted that it is like 'trying to reproduce a painting by Constable on the blackboard, or do justice to a Beethoven symphony on a mouth organ.'[16]

The Bible reveals God as One who is unchangeable and living. It is impossible to represent him by 'an image that will not move'.[17] The thought behind this description of an idol is that it needs a firm base so that the wind cannot blow it over! Furthermore, just as men are not to represent God in this way, he has chosen not to reveal himself in this way either. This is very clear from God's method of self-disclosure in the Old Testament, as R. W. Dale observed:

> God wished to be thought of by the Jews as he had revealed himself in his words and his acts . . . Throughout their history he sent them — not painters or sculptors — but prophets.[18]

There is still a further reason why we need not be surprised at Paul's reaction to the idols of Athens. Idolatry had long been associated with gross forms of sexual immorality and perversion. Paul lays considerable stress on this in the first chapter of his letter to the Romans.[19] The degrading practices he mentions are seen as a natural consequence of idolatry. Here is how C. K. Barrett describes the connection between the two:

> In the obscene pleasures to which he refers is to be seen precisely that perversion of the created order which may be expected when men put the creation in place of the Creator.[20]

This was particularly true of Canaanite religion in which even the worship itself involved sexual orgies, and the fertility cults were accompanied by practices of the most degrading kind. When heathen idolatry was imported into Israelite religion it brought these corruptions with it. This is a telling example of the way the belief and worship affect conduct.

When Paul surveyed the scene in Athens he would hardly have failed to observe that idolatry there had the same corrupt associations. There were some repulsive examples for him to see and, as E. M. Blaiklock has pointed out, there are remnants still to be seen today:

> Perhaps the Christian can still touch the edge of that deep sensation only in the revolting presence of the phallic image. Some fragments, vast and intricately carved on Delos, reveal the gross mingling of carnality and religion which stirred the wrath of the Hebrew prophets, and which evoke a Christian disgust. The sculptured sensualities of some Eastern temples stir the same nausea. Athens must have had examples enough of this baser use of Greek art.[21]

It is often said that art reflects, as it should, the outlook and spirit of its age. Paul knew that this was true of what was before him. Athens was just like any other city of those days, full of corruption and vice. Because of their ignorance of God, as he told the Ephesians, people 'have become callous and have given themselves up to licentiousness, greedy to practise every kind of uncleanness.'[22] And here before him were art forms that declared these tragic facts.

When Paul arrived in Athens then, before he uttered a word to any of its people, Athens said something to him. The works of art which surrounded him were reminders that here were people in utter ignorance of God, whose only idea of him was limited to the distorted representations of gods and goddesses of men's imagination. Coupled with this was a way of life which simply underlined their lost condition.

Today we know only too well that art in the twentieth century conveys the same message. Its plays, films, novels and songs are constantly complaining of man's lost condition, as he struggles to find some meaning to life. Christians and other decent minded people are often appalled at the increasing amount of violence and obscenity being portrayed on stage and screen. But again this is society's admission even if unwitting of its desperate spiritual condition.

Now what was Paul's response to this message about the life of Athens? Was it restricted to feelings of indignation? No, Luke tells us that it was as a direct result of what Paul had seen that he went out into Athens with the very Gospel for such a pagan society.

3

In the Market Place

The next verse in Luke's account brings before us the method the Apostle followed in his evangelistic work in Athens which, as we have seen, arose out of his reaction to the spiritual and moral condition of the city, which were conveyed to him through the art forms that he had seen —

> So he argued in the synagogue with the Jews and the devout persons, and in the market place every day with those who chanced to be there.[1]

In keeping with his usual practice, Paul made a start at the synagogue with the Jews and Gentiles who had been attracted to the Jewish religion ('the devout persons' as Luke describes them). Although we are not supplied with any details, we assume that he followed his usual approach, when presumably he was invited to speak. We have an example of this at the beginning of the same chapter, where Luke gives us a fair idea of the line Paul took in the synagogue at Thessalonica. He could assume an acceptance of the Old Testament Scriptures, so he 'argued with them from the Scriptures'. His purpose was to demonstrate that those Scriptures anticipated that the Messiah (or 'Christ' to use the Greek equivalent of the Hebrew) would suffer and then rise from the dead, and that far from this being a contradiction of Messiahship as the Jews assumed, it was 'necessary for the Christ to suffer and to rise from the dead'. He then proceeded to identify the Christ of Old Testament expectation with Jesus whom he proclaimed. Luke observes that this occupied Paul for three successive Sabbaths.[2]

Now this approach is basically identical with that of Peter in Jerusalem on the Day of Pentecost. Paul here was reaping what had previously been sown as he appealed to the Scriptures for support of his points. It was enough for him to affirm the truth with 'The Bible says . . .' Also he was conducting this ministry in the context of prayer and worship and in the place where the people of God met for worship. Here are clear similarities to much of the reaping type of evangelism that we know today.

Paul, however, was deeply aware that he was the Apostle to the Gentiles and that the pagan world outside needed his Gospel. So we are not surprised that he then turned his attention to the pagan population of Athens. But how did he set about reaching them? Surely the simple point to stress is that he went out to where they were, first in the market place and finishing up on Mars Hill. He did not organise an evangelistic service in the synagogue, and invite the Athenians to come in, even supposing that the Jewish authorities had permitted it. Nor did he hand out song sheets with the Psalms and other Jewish or Christian poems and try to conduct the Athenians in singing them to the latest hit tunes of Athens! (Why should Zeus have all the best music?) Still less did he ask them either in the market place or on Mars Hill to bow their heads for a word of prayer!

Now all this sounds obvious enough for pagan Athens, but what about pagan Britain or America? The way that we have been accustomed to thinking has meant that the word 'evangelism' almost inevitably conveys the picture of an evangelistic meeting and the evangelist as the man who conducts it. It may not necessarily be a 'guest service' in a church on a Sunday evening, but take place on 'neutral ground' such as a town hall, marquee or stadium. And yet for all that it is essentially a service. The congregation have to sing hymns in which they praise God for truths which the unbelievers, who are supposed to have been brought in, neither understand nor believe as yet. There is usually a prayer in which, quite often the non-Christians present are prayed for. (Incidentally, this can be quite an embarrassing experience for a reserved Southern Englishman, who has plucked up courage to invite his highly respectable next-door neighbour to accompany him to a religious meeting; then with his guest beside him to have to sit through a prayer for 'the unsaved who have been brought in tonight'! I have known this happen on more than one occasion. One very red-faced Christian, who had suffered in this way, once confided to me after the meeting that he felt like crawling under his chair. I must say, it made me long for the collects of the Anglican Prayer Book, 1662, notwithstanding!)

We feel bound to question whether this style of evangelism is really suitable for reaching pagans as opposed to those who think they are Christians. I have heard non-Christians reveal their impression that the hymn singing was for the purpose of softening up the audience. Others have confessed to being bored by the whole proceeding. In the days when I used to speak at open-air meetings on the promenade at Eastbourne during my curacy there in the early fifties, it was possible to draw a fair-sized crowd by straightforward preaching of the Gospel. It was noticeable, however, that whenever a hymn was announced the passers-by standing at the back of the crowd would invariably move on. A prayer would have the same effect, and Paul would no doubt have found the same in Athens. Yet many of the Christians who supported the meetings seemed to feel that to drop either was a compromise.

It is surprising, though, how many Christians are wedded to the idea of an evangelist as someone who conducts evangelistic meetings of a devotional nature. I have been taken to task for not having prayer at an evangelistic gathering I was addressing, although I protested that I had prayed with the organisers in another room before we started. I also suspected that some of the non-Christians present (and there was an encouraging number) would have felt it inappropriate to them.

I had a similar experience when conducting evangelistic missions in American universities some years ago. They took place in secular buildings and were advertised as lectures. As I was simply setting forth the 'evangel', seeking to persuade my hearers of its truth and urging them to commit themselves to Jesus Christ, I thought that what I was doing could be fairly described as evangelism. Yet the absence of hymn singing led by a large choir and many of the other familiar accompaniments of evangelistic rallies, made it difficult for some of my observers to regard me as involved in what they thought of as evangelism. Here are the comments of two university newspapers:

> Most Americans seem surprised when the Reverend Kenneth F. W. Prior says he is an evangelist. There is nothing of Elmer Gantry in this . . . man who says that an evangelist is 'anyone who presents the truth about Jesus Christ and his claims on the lives of men and women'.

Then there was an editorial which began, 'Although the Reverend Kenneth F. W. Prior calls his preaching evangelism . . .' and which encouragingly concluded,

> You won't find a 300-voice choir or mass conversions at his lectures this week, but you will encounter an evangelism that is forthright and intellectually honest, rare attractions in the circus world of American evangelism.

I would certainly not want to identify myself with many of the comments in the article, nor with this sweeping innuendo about 'the circus world of American evangelism', of which I have had little experience. It does, however, demonstrate how far some have wandered in their understanding from the simple essentials of true evangelism in the New Testament.

Surely one of the clear features of Paul's approach was that he went out to where the people were, instead of trying first to persuade them on to his ground before he shared the Gospel with them. And this seems to be forced upon us increasingly in these days. In most districts, of Britain at any rate, it is very difficult to get most people to come out to meetings, whether in a church, hall or marquee. It has become by no means a rare experience to speak at an 'evangelistic meeting', and preach one's heart out, and to discover that there isn't a single non-Christian present. It is like fishing in a bathing pool!

Ours is not the first generation of Christians to have this difficulty. George Whitefield discovered in the eighteenth century that some of those he longed to reach with the Gospel would never enter a church to hear it. So the only way was to go out into the open-air and preach there. Some would say that open-air meetings at street corners are no longer effective as they once were, and the way to reach people where they are is to go into their homes. Whatever the actual method the principle which we learn from Paul, not only from his time in Athens but from his entire missionary career, is that the way to reach people is not to expect them to come to us, but for us to go to them.

Being a pioneer made other demands upon him which are very different from what we expect of an evangelist today. There was no existing church or group of churches in Athens or most of the other cities he visited to invite him to come and conduct a series of meetings. Nor were there any local Christians to whom he could look to prepare for his arrival and invite their friends and neighbours to come and hear him. Rather it was the evangelist himself who was first on the scene and who had to go out and make his own contacts. And it was in the ability to do this, that the gifts of the evangelist largely lay.

Admittedly this is where our present society is not quite as pagan as the situation that faced Paul, since most districts have an existing church which can invite an evangelist to come and help. Yet even then, the really difficult task for which God's help is especially needed is not to find someone who can come and deliver evangelistic sermons — quite a number can do that — but to find those who can make effective contact with unbelievers wherever they are. If we insist on having meetings addressed by an evangelist, the major task will still be to persuade people to come and hear him.

Paul, however, instead of looking for an audience to come, or be brought to hear him, went out to them and spoke to them where they were. An obvious choice for this was the market place, not only because a fair crowd of people would be found there, but because this was the place where it was common practice to discuss religious and philosophical matters, as prominent thinkers like Socrates had done.

For the way that Paul addressed the people in the market place Luke uses a distinctive word. He tells us that Paul 'argued'. And lest we fail to appreciate the significance of this, we should note there is here no isolated example of Paul presenting his case in this manner. Not only does Luke frequently use the word 'argue' of his evangelistic ministry,[3] but he also has other words of similar meaning such as 'confound', 'prove',[4] 'dispute',[5] and 'powerfully confute'.[6] Expressions like this can leave us in no doubt about Paul's normal aim which was to convince people's minds of the truth of the Gospel as means of persuading them to submit their wills.

In this, Paul's method is in keeping with the place given to the mind in the whole of Scripture. Everywhere the appeal is primarily to the mind and understanding, whether it is Old Testament historian, poet or prophet, or New Testament Apostle. Also it applies to the entire Christian life. To begin with, apostate Israel was called upon to entertain the Gospel of forgiveness with the appeal, 'Come now, let reason together, says the Lord . . .'[7] Prophets, Apostles and Jesus himself call upon men to come to God in repentance, and this means literally a change of mind. If a person has come to God in this way, he will then make progress in the Christian life 'by the renewal, of his mind'.[8] He sees the warfare in which he is engaged as essentially a battle for the mind:

> The weapons of our warfare are not worldly but have divine power to destroy strongholds. We destroy arguments and every proud obstacle to the knowledge of God, and take every thought captive to obey Christ.[9]

And then when it comes to the challenge to witness before unbelievers, it is to 'be ready always to give an answer to every man that asketh you a *reason* of the hope that is in you.'[10]

Now one cannot avoid the impression that not every modern evangelist has made quite the same effort to convince people's minds of the truth of Christianity. Indeed I remember reading some years ago in a book by a fairly prominent evangelist, the remarkable statement that emotion is the driving force of the Gospel! He produced no Scriptural backing for this assertion, which was presumably based on experience of his own methods. Sometimes there has been a conscious reluctance to appeal to the mind out of an awareness that head knowledge won't save a person. We readily agree. The will must be submitted to the claims of Christ. But no one can do this without knowledge of the Gospel, and how, in view of the way that God has created us, do we know anything except with our heads? 'No one was ever argued into the Kingdom of God', it has often been said. Quite so, if this means that human argument alone is insufficient, and if the argument is allowed to become heated it will probably be a hindrance. But that does not free us from the obligation to use reasoned argument. Man has been created with a mind and God expects him to use it in understanding the truth which he has made known.

The reason why human argument alone is insufficient to bring unbelievers to a knowledge of God's truth, is that sin has distorted their minds. As a result, apart from the intervention of the Holy Spirit, they are not just waiting until the first Christian comes along to explain the Gospel and tell them why it is true, before they capitulate to its claims. Paul himself knew only too well what lay at the root of their difficulties: 'In their case the god of this world has blinded the minds of the unbelievers, to keep them from seeing the light of the Gospel . . .'[11] Such a condition demands more than a human remedy and so the ultimate cause why some have seen the truth of the Gospel is the God who said, 'Let light shine out of darkness,' who has shone in our hearts to give the light of the knowledge of the glory of God in the face of Jesus Christ.[12]

How does God bring this about? By ignoring our fallen minds and appealing instead to our feelings and emotions? There is little future in that course since they are just as fallen as our minds. God's way is not to by-pass the understanding, but to enlighten it. Indeed, in the above quotation Paul likens the illumination of a fallen mind to the first time that light penetrated the primeval darkness at the creation. Add to this the way that Paul describes the condition of the unbelieving Gentiles as living

in the futility of their minds; they are darkened in their understanding, alienated from the life of God because of the ignorance that is in them, due to their hardness of heart.[13]

What had happened to his Ephesian readers that made them so different from the other Gentiles? Something had happened to their minds. Here is how Paul describes it: 'You did not so *learn* Christ! — assuming that you have heard about him and were *taught* in him, as the truth is in Jesus.'[14] And the way to continue from such a beginning is to 'put off your old nature' and 'put on the new nature' and 'be renewed in the spirit of your minds'.[15] God, then, does not ignore people's minds and neither should we. Here is how J. I. Packer has summarised it:

The duty of Christian witness involves reasoning, as the descriptions of Paul's missionary activity show. Faith is not created by reasoning, but neither is it created without it. There is more involved in witness to Christ than throwing pre-arranged clumps of texts at unbelieving heads; the meaning and application of the gospel must be explained to men and women in terms of their actual situation. This requires hard thinking.[16]

As we shall see later, the explaining of the gospel 'to men and women in terms of their actual situation' was precisely what Paul did in Athens.

Now it must be admitted that this emphasis on the place of the mind does confront us with a problem in the twentieth century. Whether we like it or not, reasoned argument is not the usual way in which the masses of people are influenced today. Take for example advertising which plays a big part in our lives. The way in which it conditions the outlook of people and affects their choices, is characterised by a complete lack of any appeal to reason. The television commercial, to take one of the most influential forms of advertising, never employs any rational argument for preferring one brand of a product to all others. Instead, the advertiser plays on the fears and insecurities of the viewing public, and seeks to create the longings which a particular product is supposed to satisfy. The young woman who uses a particular brand of toothpaste is surrounded by male admirers. That toothpaste is primarily for the purpose of cleaning teeth seems to be beside the point! Then a virile looking young man comes on to the screen, just the kind of person the young male viewer dreams of being. And what is the secret? Of course it is the brand of beer he is drinking as he leans nonchalantly against the counter. Politics seems increasingly to follow the same tack. General elections are to a large extent won or lost by the kind of image created by the party leader, and his television performance plays a large part in this. Vance Packard in his penetrating study of the techniques of modern advertising writes of it in these terms:

> The use of mass psychoanalysis to guide campaigns of persuasion has become the basis of a multi-million-dollar industry. Professional persuaders have seized upon it in their groping for more effective ways to sell us their

wares — whether products, ideas, attitudes, candidates, goals
or states of mind.[17]

How is the Christian persuader going to set about convincing
people that the Gospel he offers is true, will work and is just
what they need? Is he to assault them with the techniques we
have described? If he is a conductor of campaigns he certainly
has some opportunity to do so. He can advertise his work so as
to build up his image. If he can draw a crowd there are ways in
which he can manipulate them. Adolf Hitler was a genius at
this and discovered what he could do with a stadium full of
young people by getting them to chant repeatedly, *'Ein Volk,
ein Reich, ein Führer'*. An evangelist can use repetitive and
rhythmical singing with the same effect. Sentimentality in the
choice of music and illustrations can produce 'results', but we
feel entitled to ask whether there are real conversions produced
in this way.

Needless to say these and other ways of by-passing the intellect have no place in Scripture. The appeal is always first to the
mind with a view to the will being challenged to respond. The
emotions such as fear, love, joy and wonder might well be
aroused, but it is as a result of being convinced about the truth
and not vice versa. This does not have to involve us in long and
intricate reasoning. There is nothing to suggest that Paul's ar-
guing in the market place was of this kind either. He may well
have given them small doses and been content to take his
hearers a short distance at a time as he did with the uneducated
farming community in Acts 14. Nor do we have to indulge in
abstract philosophical notions. Most people think in concrete
terms. Our Lord made use of copious illustrations, mostly from
nature and agriculture, when speaking to the crowds. We know
from Paul's writings that he too could use analogy.

These provisos, however, do not mean that we by-pass the
intellect. Rather, it is part of a Christian's witness to expose the
irrationality of today's world. If God has created us with minds
then he intends us to use them. And this is the way by which he

expects us to find him and be led by him. Here is how the Psalmist put it:

> I will instruct you and teach you
> the way you should go;
> I will counsel you with my eye upon you.
> Be not like a horse or mule, without understanding.[18]

If we are to argue our case effectively, not only do we need to be masters of what we believe and why, but we also must appreciate the outlook and problems of those we are trying to reach. Otherwise we are in very real danger of talking at cross purposes, and failure to observe this principle of communication may well lie at the heart of some of our difficulties in evangelism today. But Paul did not fall into this mistake, as will now become apparent.

4

Chance or Fate?

We must now proceed to consider the implications of a very significant detail which Luke gives us: 'Some also of the Epicurean and Stoic philosophers met him.'[1] Now why should Luke bother to include this piece of information?

During recent years, the thinking of many Christians has been influenced by Francis Schaeffer. Whether or not one goes all the way with his views, it is difficult to resist the good sense of his general approach. Here is how he describes it as he begins his first book:

> If a man goes overseas for any length of time we would expect him to learn the language of the country to which he is going. More than this is needed, however, if he is really to communicate with the people among whom he is living. He must learn another language — that of the thought forms of the people to whom he speaks. Only then will he have real communication with them and to them. So it is with the Christian Church. Its responsibility is not only to hold to the basic, scriptural principles of the Christian faith, but to communicate these unchanging truths 'into' the generation in which it is living.[2]

Schaeffer's book is then devoted to the philosophical ideas and their history which lie behind the outlook and thinking of people today.

Now the Epicurean and Stoic philosophies were like that. Their influence on the general outlook of the day was considerable. And when we come to the Areopagus address itself we shall discover that Paul had taken the trouble to understand the thinking of his hearers. Especially is there every indication that he appreciated the shortcomings of both systems of philosophy.

Our Lord in his ministry to individuals showed the same sensitivity to the problems of the people he was seeking to help. The classical example is the way he dealt with the Samaritan woman in John 4. His approach to her was shaped not only by the truth that he wished to convey, but also by the problems arising both from her background as a Samaritan and from the particular sins of which she was guilty. This meant that he had no cut and dried method for all and sundry, but rather, his approach varied from one individual to another. This also applied to his healing ministry which affords some striking examples. One is the man who suffered from deafness and an impediment in his speech. Those who brought him to Jesus assumed that he would simply 'lay his hands upon him', as they had seen him do with others. But Jesus was not tied to any fixed methods. Instead he perceived that in order to awaken faith in a man who suffered from deafness as well as a speech defect a different form of treatment was called for.[3]

In the light of this we ought to examine modern methods of personal evangelism, which prescribe a set of points to be almost mechanically applied to the potential convert. No provision is made for listening to what the unbeliever has to say, with a view to understanding his problems and discovering the point at which the Gospel applies to his need. Now admittedly if a Christian perseveres with a stereotyped approach he is likely to meet with some success, as sooner or later he will presumably encounter someone to whom the way in which he presents the Gospel applies. Furthermore, knowing what we do about the sovereign grace of God, we may expect him to see to it that a completely dedicated evangelist will be rewarded by a contact which fits his approach. Also, we have no doubt, that these methods are often of great help to the Christian in impressing upon his mind the basic points of the Gospel. What our present study demands of us is that we should add to these basic essentials a greater awareness of the outlook of those we are trying to reach, and, as a consequence, apply them in a more flexible manner.

This is where the approach of present-day writers like Michael Green score so heavily. Take, for example, his book on the evidence for the Resurrection, *Man Alive*. Here he employs most of the traditional arguments, but he applies them to the futility of the outlook of many today, which he describes in his opening chapter which is headed, 'More dead than alive'. He demonstrates that in the spiritual death that is apparent in modern society, the 'modern predicament' is not essentially different from the 'ancient predicament', to use his sub-headings. Into this context he introduces his theme which, as we shall see, is essentially that of Paul in Athens, 'Jesus and the resurrection'.[4]

Some may wonder what the Epicurean and Stoic philosophies had to do with many of the people Paul encountered in the market place. Not all of those he spoke with would have been versed in philosophy, and the way in which he was misunderstood by a section of his hearers, who thought he was offering them two extra deities, suggests that some of them at least were not outstandingly bright![5] The Areopagus address itself was presumably confined to the intelligentsia of Athens, who would have known all about these philosophies. The same could be asked about the relevance of taking into account the speculations of modern thinkers, when contemplating the evangelisation of the semi-educated masses today.

Such questions stem from a failure to appreciate the influence of philosophical systems. The two to which Luke draws our attention may at first sight seem far removed from the popular religion of Athens which was represented by the crude forms of idolatry that affected Paul. Yet their influence was by no means confined to the frequenters of libraries. Indeed, as we shall see, these two philosophies lie at the heart of masses of ordinary people today. The same can be said of more recent examples. Names like Hegel and Kierkegaard have probably never been heard of by the vast majority of people. Yet the way of thinking that has developed through them is everywhere, in the mass media, art, popular culture and so on.

So we now turn to a brief description of the Epicurean and Stoic philosophies.

The former is named after Epicurus, whose dates were 341–270 BC. He is best known for his view of ethics, that 'good' is simply what brings most pleasure. The utilitarianism of John Stuart Mill is a nineteenth century refinement of this position, where the aim becomes 'the greatest happiness of the greatest number'. The pursuit of happiness as an end in itself is the purpose which dominates the lives of a vast number of people today. You are free to do just what you like ('your own thing') provided that it does not interfere with the happiness of anyone else.

Lying behind this was the theological view of Epicurus. He was not strictly speaking an atheist, but to all intents and purposes he might have been, because he taught that the gods, whatever they may have done in creating the world, have no further interest in it. All that happens now simply comes about by chance. There is no life beyond the grave as death ends everything. There is ultimately nothing to fear and nothing to hope for. As far as this life is concerned their motto could well be, as Paul would have put it, 'eat, drink and be merry, for tomorrow we die', although to be fair to Epicurus and his immediate followers, they did not pursue these views to this, their logical conclusion.

It is not difficult to see that this stress on chance underlies the outlook of multitudes of people in the twentieth century, although few of them will have heard of Epicurus. Everything is the result of 'luck'. If their affairs have not been going well, they are 'down on their luck', while every Friday queues form in Post Offices all over Britain of people buying postal orders which they religiously send off with their football pool coupons in the distant hope of a 'lucky break' which will change their fortune overnight.

Side by side with those who held these views were the Stoics. Their ideas were first propounded by Zeno (335–263 BC), although they are also associated with others who produced their own modifications. What their position amounts to is this. The affairs of the world are directed by a blind, impersonal but rational force within it, sometimes called a 'world-soul'. This view is quite common in the twentieth century, only instead of 'world-soul' people speak of 'Nature', spelling it with a capital 'N', as the force at work in creation. Theologians would describe this view as 'pantheistic'. Although this can have a variety of forms, it basically holds that God is wholly immanent in the world. Whether he is identified with creation, or contained within it, there is nothing of God outside of it.

Like every view of life, Stoicism has a way of living based upon it. The most satisfactory way to live is not to struggle against one's circumstances but accept things as they are. In so doing you ally yourself to the inherent Reason, as they called it, within the universe. You must not allow your emotions to take control, but you must ensure that your life is always subject to reason. This is the way of peace of mind and contentment.

This attitude to life made a strong appeal to the Roman mind, and it numbered some prominent names among its adherents, such as the emperor, Marcus Aurelius. It is clearly the complete opposite of the Epicurean approach. Instead of being ruled by chance, the happenings in the world are determined by fate, and a cold, impersonal and merciless thing it is. Men often turn to fatalism when life is difficult. Accepting things as they are with reason and without emotion is often called the way of the 'stiff upper lip'. It flourishes in wartime when you resign yourself to the view that if the bullet or the bomb 'has got your name on it', it will get you whatever you do. More recently I saw on television a succession of passers-by being asked if they intended to give up smoking in view of the hazard to health it entails. A surprising number replied that they would not, because if you are going to die soon you will die anyway. If not through lung cancer, you will probably be run over in the street, so why worry? One cannot deny that such an outlook has had its uses if you can sustain it![6]

Now the observation which has an important bearing on our theme, is that these two systems represent the only two alternatives to the personal God of Biblical revelation. If you don't believe that in the last analysis the affairs of this world are ordered by a personal God who is quite distinct from his creatures and yet has a personal relationship with them, what else is there? One alternative is that the Universe, the earth, life and human personality and all that befalls them are one gigantic fluke. The other option is that there is some impersonal force at work. As far as our present lives are concerned, either they are at the mercy of a frivolous thing called chance, or in the pitiless grip of a cold impersonal fate.

These issues tend to become prominent when the problem of suffering is under discussion. A Christian often finds himself hard put to it to explain it in terms of a personal God. But what are the alternatives? Whether suffering arises from chance or fate, either way, there is no hope.

The comment of Professor F. F. Bruce aptly summarises the position:

Stoicism and Epicureanism represent alternative attempts in pre-Christian paganism to come to terms with life, especially in times of uncertainty and hardship, and post-Christian paganism has not been able to devise anything appreciably better.[7]

5

Jesus and the Resurrection

Having drawn our attention to the two schools of thought represented among Paul's hearers, Luke proceeds to describe the way in which Paul's efforts on the market place were received. We shall pay attention to this in our next chapter, but before that we ought to discover what Paul argued about, and to pick up the thread we left at the end of chapter three.

Now Luke does not give us many details about this, but the little that he does reveal is very significant indeed. Paul's main emphasis comes out very clearly from the way his hearers' reactions are described. So to return to Luke's account:

> And some said, 'What would this babbler say?' Others said, 'He seems to be a preacher of foreign divinities' — because he preached Jesus and the resurrection.[1]

There may have been other Gospel truths to which he referred, but according to the impression gained by many in his audience, these were the two basic facts that lay at the heart of his argument for the truth of Christianity — 'Jesus and the resurrection'.

The person of Christ lay at the centre of all the Apostolic preaching recorded in the Acts, not least that of Paul himself. Immediately after his conversion we find him in Damascus 'proving that Jesus was the Christ'.[2] Right through his ministry he maintained the same emphasis. Only just before his visit to Athens he had spent three weeks in Thessalonica during which he spoke at the local synagogue on each Sabbath day and argued with them from the scriptures, explaining and proving that it was necessary for the Christ to suffer and to rise from the dead, and saying, 'This Jesus, whom I proclaim to you is the Christ'.[3]

At the end of the Acts he is still at it, 'trying to convince them about Jesus'.[4]

In Athens, so it seems, he had the same theme. Once he had left the synagogue where he began, and was among the Gentiles in the market place, we would not expect him to prove that Jesus was the Christ of Old Testament prophecy. Nor did he do so at Lystra in Acts 14, the other occasion when he was addressing an exclusively Gentile audience. In the early chapters of his letter to the Romans it is most noticeable that when addressing Gentiles from 1:18 to 2:16 he makes no Old Testament quotations, although he does so from 2:17 onwards when he is addressing the Jews. In the Areopagus address, it is true, there are marks of Old Testament teaching, but nowhere does he appeal to its authority to enforce what he is saying. So what does he do in the market place? Even though he does not identify him with the Christ anticipated in the Old Testament, he still argues about Jesus.

This has always been a hall mark of true evangelism — the centrality of the person of Jesus Christ. How often John Wesley recorded in his diary, 'I came into the town and offered them Christ'. It is the reason why John's Gospel has so often been used to good effect in evangelism, especially among those who have been avowed unbelievers, for this is its declared purpose. The writer himself explains that this aim governed his choice of material from the many miracles and discourses at his disposal from the life of Christ:

Now Jesus did many other signs in the presence of his disciples, which are not written in this book; but these are written that you may believe that Jesus is the Christ, the Son of God, and that believing you may have life through his name.[5]

Some years ago the Church of England produced a report, *Towards the Conversion of England.* It included some excellent suggestions, especially for the days in which it was written. Unfortunately it did little more than provide material for discussion groups among church people before it was finally shelved. Here is a paragraph from that report which shows how Bishop Linton applied what he had proved among Moslems of the value of Christ-centred evangelism to the neo-pagans of his diocese of Birmingham:

> Bishop Hensley Henson recalls how he asked Bishop Linton, 'the most successful evangelist of Moslems that our church possesses . . . what he found to be the element in Christianity which appealed most to the Mohammedans in Persia.' The answer was that 'it was the person and character of Christ, *not* conviction of sin. The sense of sin developed in converts, but it played no part in their conversion.' Bishop Linton finds the same equally true in Birmingham.[6]

At this stage there is a caution that ought to be sounded in view of the way that 'Jesus' has become a popular figure in recent times, even to the extent of being a character suitable for the stage. We need constantly to ask whether the 'Jesus' being presented is the Jesus of the New Testament in whom Paul and the other Apostles believed. This danger was by no means unknown to Paul, because he warned the church at Corinth that among the errors they must guard against is the teaching of anyone who 'comes and preaches another Jesus than the one we preached.'[7] To the Colossians, who were being presented with a Jesus who fitted the notions of Greek philosophy, he gave the reminder that the Jesus he preached was one 'in whom the whole fullness of deity dwells bodily.'[8]

I well remember applying these warnings to Dennis Potter's *Son of Man* when watching it on television a few years ago. I really could not imagine anyone saying to his version of Jesus, 'You have the words of eternal life'.[9] Still less would anyone have acclaimed him 'the Christ, the Son of the living God'.[10] It was difficult to resist the conclusion that the whole play was a deliberate attempt to reduce Jesus to the size that suits the presuppositions of those who deny the supernatural.

Now the Jesus of the New Testament will not fit the limits of such thinking. He made uncompromising claims about himself, such as the power to forgive sins and to give eternal life. He declared that one day he will appear again as the judge of the whole world. With God he claimed a unique relationship. This was also the Jesus that Paul preached, and that this was the main direction of his argument in Athens may be inferred from the impression of some of his hearers that he was setting up Jesus as another deity.

The other emphasis in Paul's argument which made an impact upon his hearers was the resurrection. This too was constantly on the lips of the Apostles when they were testifying to the truth of the Gospel. The reason why they were so sure that it was a fact of history was simply that they were witnesses of the event, as they repeatedly claimed.[11] Paul makes it quite clear that he too was well aware of this apostolic witness of the resurrection.[12] Indeed he gives a detailed account of it to the church at Corinth, and actually numbers himself among the witnesses, regarding his conversion experience on the Damascus road in this way.[13] To the early Christians the resurrection was the supreme evidence of the truth of Christianity. This was the sign to which Jesus had pointed when he refused to give other signs.[14]

Now it seems not unreasonable to conclude that this was how Paul was using the resurrection in Athens when he linked it with the person of Jesus. He made the same connection when writing to the Romans pointing out that Jesus was 'designated Son of God in power ... by his resurrection from the dead.'[15]

That Paul was using the fact of the resurrection to confirm the truth of Christianity is further indicated by the way he returns to it right at the end of the Areopagus address. Here

Paul underlines the certainty of what he has been saying by affirming of it that God 'has given assurance to all men by raising him from the dead.'[16]

This then is his own explanation of what he has been speaking about in the market place, when he argued about 'Jesus and the resurrection'.

An obvious question to ask is how we follow the Apostle's example in using the fact of the resurrection to establish the truth of what we believe about Jesus and the Gospel. The problem is that unlike the first Christians, we have not had the advantage of seeing the risen Christ with our physical eyes. How then can this witness to the resurrection have an impact on unbelieving minds today? The way that some Christians get over this difficulty is to offer instead a very different kind of witness from the Apostles, feeling understandably that this is all they can do. Their answer to an enquirer could be expressed in the words of a well-known couplet:

You ask me how I know he lives?
He lives within my heart.

In other words for the apostles' witness to the resurrection as an objective, historical fact, they substitute a subjective, inward experience.

Those who use this kind of language may find themselves in unexpected company, because this is the approach of those modern exponents who share the views of Rudolf Bultmann. The difference is that the latter would go further and disclaim all interest in whether the resurrection was an event in history at all. What matters is a present experience of the risen Christ, and this, so they say, does not depend on whether the body of Jesus was left to decay in the tomb or not. Paul clearly thought otherwise, and with all due respects to modern theologians, some of us, at least, still regard him as a more reliable guide as to what is essential to the Christian faith. What Paul says in the following, for example, is somewhat different from the idea that it does not matter whether or not Christ rose again provided you enjoy an experience of his risen life:

> If Christ has not been raised, then our preaching is in vain and your faith is in vain. We are even found to be mis-representing God, because we testified of God that he raised Christ, whom he did not raise if it is true that the dead are not raised ... If Christ has not been raised, your faith is futile and you are still in your sins.[17]

It is worth noting that the New Testament Christians never attempted to establish the truth of Christianity on their inward experiences. Other people certainly took note of the change in their lives, but that is a different matter. Also we may be sure that they would not have rested content with the resurrection simply as a fact of bare history. Paul claimed that the risen life of Christ was part of his experience when, for example, he declared, 'Christ lives in me'.[18] That, however, does not mean that he ever advanced this experience as the ground on which others ought to believe. To put it another way, never do we find him trying to prove the truth of Christianity to others 'because of the difference it has made to my life'.

Appealing to our experiences is open to a serious objection in that other faiths and cults do the same. A short time ago I heard the testimony of a young man to the deep sense of peace and joy he had found. His language reminded me of that used by many a young evangelical. He was referring, however, to what he had found through a mystical Eastern religion. There was no reason to doubt the validity of the experience he claimed, but that did not establish the truth of the doctrines on which it was based.

What is the lesson in all this for Christians today? It is surely that our primary task is not to press upon others our own ex-perience, important though this may be to ourselves, but rather to expose them to the testimony of the Apostles to the resur-rection as an historical event. It is they who were God's chosen witnesses as Peter claimed:

God raised him on the third day and made him manifest; not to all the people but to us who were chosen by God as witnesses, who ate and drank with him after he rose from the dead.[19]

This was the ground on which Jesus himself expected Christians subsequent to the original apostles to believe. In his prayer for his disciples he prayed not only for the existing ones who had witnessed his earthly ministry and were about to witness his resurrection, but 'also for those who believe in me through their word.'[20]

It may well be asked how we do this 2000 years after the apostles lived. The answer is that we have the claims they made for Jesus, both his person and resurrection, in the writings they have left us. The unbeliever may be unwilling to share the Christian belief that these writings, are inspired and constitute the 'Word of God', but they are, for all that, the writings of the first Christians, and the claims they make still demand an answer.

Bultmann, in the cause of his so-called demythologising, makes the assertion, 'All that historical criticism can establish is the fact that the first disciples came to believe in the resurrection.'[21] But this is also an admission. It is that we can be sure that the disciples did, in fact, claim that Jesus rose from the dead. The challenge this presents to the unbelieving mind, whether ancient or modern, is to determine the origin of that belief. Was it based on fact, or was it all a delusion? Paul saw no reason for shielding the secular minds of his day from this choice, so why should we today? It has sometimes been suggested that the all-important difference between that age and our own, is that we are now in a scientific age. Are we to imagine from this, then, that in a pre-scientific age it was easier to accept the bodily resurrection of our Lord than it is today? There is no evidence that it was. Paul knew that the claims he was making would stretch their credulity, and the fact that he persisted in making them only goes to show how certain he felt of his facts. It is no different today. The rise of modern physics has not made it more or less easy to accept a supernatural event like the resurrection.

We have to face, of course, that in a secular society there are many who find it difficult to believe anything supernatural. When confronted with evidence for a miraculous event like the ressurection, they have a built-in reaction which is to explain it away, and it is amazing the lengths to which some will go in doing this. There is an extreme example in what has usually been called the Swoon theory to account for the primitive belief in the resurrection. The suggestion is that Jesus did not die on the cross, but only fainted. It so happened that the authorities forgot to ensure that Jesus was dead, as they usually did with the victims of judicial crucifixion. As a consequence he was interred unconscious but still alive. Then after three days something very remarkable happened. In spite of his condition and lack of medical attention during that time, he revived. Still more remarkably, he extricated himself from the grave clothes in which he was bound from his neck down to his feet, and severely wounded though he was, he succeeded in rolling the large stone to one side, a difficult enough feat for someone in the best of health. He then sought out his disciples, who had fled in terror at his crucifixion, and convinced them that he had risen from the dead. Jesus then conveniently disappeared from the scene. This has been advanced as a serious explanation! It only demonstrates how eager some have been to avoid anything supernatural.

And what we have just described is by no means the only evasion that has been tried. Another is the suggestion that the New Testament narratives of the resurrection were no more than an attempt on the part of the early church to express their conviction about the triumph and exaltation of Jesus. It was just their way of saying that something remarkable had happened to Jesus.

Paul must have been aware of this kind of prejudice in his day, when he addressed King Agrippa, 'Why is it thought incredible by any of you that God raises the dead?'[22]

To those who argue that a resurrection would be an extremely unusual event, the answer is to agree. Jesus was an unusual person. If in his person God was intervening directly in the world's history, and making a special revelation of himself to man, would it not be more surprising if miracles did not occur? Of course they do not take place during the normal course of history, but the life, death and resurrection of Christ were not part of 'the normal course of history'. So the only honest approach is to examine the evidence for the resurrection with an open mind, without begging the question with the presupposition that because it was a miracle it could not have happened.

At this point it is well worth noting that many who have studied the resurrection evidences have found them convincing. Of the many books that have been written setting them out there is the one by Frank Morison who set out in the first place to write a book disproving the resurrection. He describes that, however, in the heading of his opening chapter as 'The book that refused to be written',[23] for the evidence drove him to the opposite conclusion.

It may well be asked what unbelievers, who persist in their unbelief, have to say about the resurrection. That is not an easy question to answer. To pretend that they all hold to fantastic explanations like the Swoon theory we have described would be patently unfair. What they do seem to do is to ignore it. Bertrand Russell in his book, *Why I am not a Christian* never mentions it. So we conclude that in his case, and in that of many others, it is either because of ignorance, or an example of 'running away from history'.[24]

So one of the dominant needs in evangelism is to face people with the person of Christ and the evidence for his resurrection. There are, of course, other truths which are essential to salvation, and which will be included. But when approaching those who do not share our biblical presuppositions, Paul's emphasis in Athens shows us where we can begin.[25]

6

What's New?

The way that men react to the Gospel does not necessarily tell
us anything about the Gospel, but it does reveal a great deal
about them. It is similar to a person expressing his opinion
about great works of art in an art gallery. If he declares that
some of the great paintings are not worth the canvas they are
painted on, it is not likely to have any effect on their value. All
his remarks succeed in doing is to reveal a lot about himself and
his tastes, and he would probably be dismissed as an uncultured
philistine.

So it is with men's response to the Gospel. This is amply
demonstrated in John's Gospel. The reaction of the Jews, for
example, to the healing of the man born blind and the teaching
of Jesus connected with it in John 9, simply underlines their
own spiritual blindness. Similarly we can add to our understanding of the people Paul encountered in the market place at
Athens, by considering the way in which they received his arguments.

We are first given an indication of the way in which some of
them reacted to Paul himself: 'What would this babbler
say?'[1]

This was not exactly an attractive way of referring to anyone.
A 'babbler' or 'seed-picker' was a bit of Athenian slang, and denoted originally a bird that lived on seeds and odd scraps it
managed to scavenge from the streets. It came to be used of a
man who made money by posing as a teacher of philosophy, but
who had picked up his scraps of learning from others. *Today's
English Version* renders it, 'What is this ignorant show-off

trying to say?' There seem to have been many of these people about, and they must have developed quite a skill in concealing the second-hand nature of their teaching and lack of any genuine knowledge.

Is this the familiar picture of people reading their own faults into others? When I was serving my first curacy following my ordination a few years after the end of the war, a man told me that I was in the ministry only for what I could 'get out of it'. What I was in fact getting out of it was the princely sum of £250 a year after years of training and a university degree, and out of this I had to pay everything including board and lodging. But why did my critic make this judgment about my motives? Subsequent conversation revealed quite clearly that 'what you can get out of it' was his only aim in life, and apparently he could not imagine that anyone else could be any different from himself. One cannot help wondering whether Paul's critics tacitly assumed that he had the same unworthy motives as many of them.

In the same verse we then come to another reaction which shows how they understood Paul's teaching: ' "He seems to be a preacher of foreign divinities" — because he preached Jesus and the resurrection.'[1]

Just as people will see their own faults in others, so they will often read their own presuppositions into what they say. They will listen selectively, hearing what they agree with, and ignoring any ideas which are new to them. This seems to be how some of the Athenians came to this gross misunderstanding of what Paul was trying to convey to them. Although much that he said went over their heads, or was simply ignored through lack of interest on their part, they pricked up their ears whenever he referred to 'Jesus and the resurrection'. With their long tradition of polytheism it sounded to them like a personification of 'healing' and 'restoration', which is what 'Jesus' and 'resurrection' mean in Greek, and they assumed that Paul was introducing them to two new deities, perhaps a married couple!

This is a difficulty for which we must always be on the lookout, whenever we are speaking to people with deeply ingrained assumptions. A very common example of such an assumption is the widespread idea, that if there is a God who gives any kind of salvation to men, then it must be as a reward for a good life. I have known this view to be read into a sermon which says precisely the opposite. On one occasion when this happened in my experience, I had spoken on the text, 'By grace are you saved through faith . . . not of works lest any man should boast'. I thought I had made it crystal clear that salvation is offered to us as a free gift from God by virtue of Christ's death on the cross, and is not earned by us. After the service a very respectable lady told me what a wonderful sermon it was. My understandable pleasure at such a compliment was stifled at birth however, when she added, 'It is just what my late husband used to say, do your best and God will look after you'!

Sometimes we can unwittingly court problems of this kind out of a genuine desire to make the Gospel relevant to people by using their language. Some, when speaking against the background of the drug scene, have used language like 'getting high on Jesus'. This is tantamount to asking our hearers to read their own outlook into what we are saying with the possible result that they come to regard Jesus too as a kind of drug. Many of the thought forms into which our message may well be interpreted relate to experiences of a subjective nature, because this is what so many are seeking today. Commercial advertising is full of it. A brand of tobacco is 'cool and refreshing'; a certain drink is 'satisfying'; other products such as make-up, toothpaste and deodorants give 'confidence'; while others offer what promises to be 'exhilarating' or 'exciting'. So we need not be surprised if when we speak of man's guilt, they will assume that we mean psychological guilt, rather than moral guilt before God, which is what the Bible speaks of. In this context, then, we must be careful not to over-emphasise the subjective results of being a Christian, such as the joy and peace we may look for, if we wish to avoid giving the impression that Christianity is just a piece of good psychology. After all what matters most of all is the fact of sins forgiven, more than any feelings that result from it.

There is another observation that is worth making in passing. Paul's hearers were ready enough to adapt what he said to fit their preconceived notions, but they still regarded them as '*foreign* divinities'. Now it has sometimes been maintained that the New Testament doctrine of the death and resurrection of Christ is just a christianised version of the Greek myth of the dying and rising of the nature god. If this is so, why did the Athenians not recognise Paul's teaching as such? On the contrary not only did they regard the gods they thought Paul was bringing them as 'foreign divinities', but they also assumed that what he taught was '*new* teaching', and that he was bringing '*strange* things' to their ears.[2] This hardly suggests that the Athenians thought that Paul's message had anything in common with the death-and-rebirth myths of the mystery religions. We find Paul himself making the same observation. His preaching of the death of Christ, far from being recognised as part of a familiar pagan myth in another form, was, as he put it, 'folly to the Gentiles'.[3]

Now it was the newness of Paul's teaching that proved to hold the special fascination for the Athenian mind which led to the delivery of the Areopagus address. It was a characteristic for which they were known, as Luke explains: 'Now all the Athenians and foreigners who lived there spent their time in nothing except telling or hearing some new thing.'[4] This had long been a characteristic of the Athenians. Professor F. F. Bruce draws his readers' attention to the orator Demosthenes who,

> four hundred years earlier, had reproached them for going about asking if there was any fresh news in a day when Philip of Macedon's rise to power presented a threat which called for deeds not words.[5]

The disillusionment on the part of many in the Athens of Paul's day over what was traditional, might well have been an added reason for running after novelties.

This particular characteristic of the people of Athens is well worth reflection by readers in the second half of the twentieth century, when we often find a similar searching for something new. A recent book, which is described by its publisher as 'A study of the revolution in English life in the fifties and sixties', carries the title *The Neophiliacs*. This seems to be a word specially coined for the purpose, presumably meaning, lovers of what is new. Among the groups responsible for the far-reaching changes in the period covered by the book, the author Christopher Booker discerns 'The Oxbridge "Intellectuals" and the Upper-class young'. Under this heading he comments:

> The upper classes in England had in fact been losing faith in their traditional values, and bourgeois self-confidence had been crumbling for over half a century.[6]

He then traces the swing to the left among the upper and middle classes from those of them who helped to found the Labour Party at the turn of the century, to 'the great upper-middle class swing to the left in the Thirties'. It was during this period that Oxford in particular produced the class rebels that led the search for a new freedom and vitality after the Second World War, and which further led among other things to the cult of youth that grew up in the sixties.

So disillusionment with the traditions and values of the past may be one of the reasons common to the first and twentieth centuries for 'telling or hearing some new thing'. At the same time, however, there is one very important difference. In ancient times little of any significance noticeably changed. As the years and even the centuries passed by people wore the same style of clothing, travelled by the same means, lived in the same kind of houses and fought their wars with the same type of weapons. So the search for new ideas in philosophy and religion could not be said to arise out of changes in everything else.

With the twentieth century it is very different. One of the most prominent features of the past hundred years has been the way in which everything has been changing, and hardly an aspect of human life has been exempt. Not only has the rate of change been breath-taking, but in recent years changes have been accelerating out of all proportion. Thus a present day writer can assert,

> the world of today . . . is as different from the world in which I was born as that world was from Julius Caesar's. I was born in the middle of human history, to date, roughly. Almost as much has happened since I was born as happened before.[7]

This applies to science and technology, population growth and the using up of the world's energy resources. And the changes are accelerating. Of the many examples Toffler chooses there is speed. In 1784, he reminds us, the first mail coach averaged a mere ten mph. The first steam locomotive in 1825 achieved a top speed of only thirteen mph. In the 1880s the more advanced steam locomotives reached what then seemed an enormous speed — one hundred mph — and 'It took the human race millions of years to attain that record'. Here is how Toffler continues the story:

> It took only fifty-eight years, however, to quadruple the limit, so that by 1938 airborn man was cracking the 400 mph line. It took a mere twenty year flick of time to double the limit again. And by the 1960s rocket planes approached speeds of 4,800 mph, and men in space capsules were circling the earth at 18,000 mph. Plotted on a graph, the line representing progress in the past generation would leap vertically off the page.
>
> Whether we examine distances travelled, altitudes reached, minerals mined, or explosive power harnessed, the same accelerative trend is obvious. The pattern, here and in a thousand other statistical series, is absolutely clear and un-

mistakable. Millennia or centuries go by, and then, in our own times, a sudden bursting of the limits, a fantastic spurt forward.[8]

It is not surprising that in this kind of world men are constantly expecting something new. Luxuries of the present soon cease to satisfy in the anticipation that they will shortly be surpassed by some fresh invention. Radio is no longer the novelty it once was when television arrives on the scene, and this too is further improved by colour televison. For many years clothing, for women at least, has constantly changed with new fashions every year. We live in what has come to be called a 'throw-away society' of ball-point pens which are discarded as soon as they run out, disposable towels, non-returnable bottles and so on. Although our washing machines, refrigerators, cameras and cars are fit to last for many years, commercial advertising is constantly persuading us that we need new ones and that there are better models on the market. And so we could continue with example after example of how modern man is being brain-washed into thinking that he must always be having 'something new'.

How is Christianity likely to be viewed by such a society? Will it hold out a fascination as yet something else that is new? Here, unfortunately perhaps, we have to face a difference between pre-Christian and post-Christian paganism. Today, rather than be drawn to the Gospel as 'some new thing', men are more likely to dimiss it with the quip, 'Tell me the old, old story!' Christianity, like so many other things, belongs to an inferior past which has now been superseded, and every disused or little-used church building bears eloquent testimony that this is so.

The way to attract interest in Christianity, it would seem, is to announce that one has discovered a new version which discards many of its traditional tenets. R. J. Campbell did it at the City Temple in London at the end of the last century, with the stir he created when he produced his so-called 'New Theology', and had a book published with that title. More recently John Robinson has done something similar with his *Honest to God,* which attracted wide attention. A few years ago someone told me that the way for a preacher to get into the newspapers or on to the radio, is for him to announce from his pulpit that he no longer believes in the resurrection, in saying his prayers or going to church. But what about the many who do still believe these things? I once heard a journalist explain that such ortho-doxy holds little interest because it contains 'no news value'. Apparently then, people are still like the Athenians who 'spent their time in nothing except telling or hearing something new'.

A fascination with novelties can, of course, provide openings for the Gospel and make people ready to discuss religion. There is, however, the danger of trifling with serious issues. This came home to me quite forcefully once when I was con-ducting a mission in a university. I was talking to one of the students who had responded to my invitation to seek help from a personal talk with me. As I seemed to be getting nowhere with him, I asked him why he had come to see me. He was perfectly frank. He was attending a short course in the Phil-osophy of Religion, and his tutor had recommended him to seek a personal interview with me, as he would find me an interest-ing subject for study. It was clear that I was simply being regarded as a religious phenomenon! I suspect there was some-thing of this in the Athenians' attitude to Paul. All this shows what an interesting topic religion can be, and why it is just the subject for an enjoyable discussion group. But there is a snag. Paul drew the attention of his young colleague Timothy to it when he warned him of those 'who will listen to anybody and can never arrive at a knowledge of the truth.'[9] Some people treat Christian truth like chewing gum. They will chew it over in discussion for hours, but never swallow it.

Now it was the Athenians' interest in the new ideas that Paul had brought to their city that prompted the enquiry that led to the Areopagus address. So seeking for clarification, they took hold of him and brought him to the Areopagus, saying, 'May we know what this new teaching is which you present? For you bring some strange things to our ears; we wish to know therefore what these things mean.'[10]

The Unknown God

The Court of Areopagus took its name from the hill where it met, the 'hill or Ares', or 'Mars Hill' as the older English version renders it. It was in no sense a criminal court, but was a gathering of some of the leading minds of Athens, which had a great influence and authority in matters of religion and morals. So to examine and pronounce on the new teaching brought to them by Paul was well within their terms of reference.

Paul began his address with an assessment of his hearers. This is always important for witness and evangelism in any setting. Paul's own advice is 'that you may know how you ought to answer everyone'.[1] As a result of his stroll around the city and the observations he had made, he knew just how to answer the men of Athens. He began by making two points about them. He first recognised that his hearers were basically religious, but in the same breath claimed that their religion was based on ignorance. He was able to substantiate his assessment by what he had seen in their city.

What an important principle this is! It is not enough to pour the truth into an unbelieving ear, no matter how skilfully it is done. There must be some understanding of our hearers, their problems and difficulties. This is why it is necessary to give the person we are seeking to help an opportunity to speak, if we are going to address ourselves to his need. Jesus did this and, as we saw in chapter four, he had a different approach for everyone he sought to help. Here is one of the chief objections to stereotyped methods of approach, where the whole conversation which the Christian is intended to have with anyone he is trying to win is virtually mapped out in advance. True, it is important to have a clear grasp of the basic facts of the Gospel which must be ultimately covered in leading a person to faith in Christ, but this is not the same as prescribing a detailed technique. If we are to start with people where they are, there is no line of approach which fits all cases, and there is no evidence that Paul or anyone else in the New Testament employed one either.

To return to Paul's first point, here is how he put it:

'Men of Athens, I perceive that in every way you are very religious.'[2]

The word 'religious' is rendered by 'superstitious' in the older English versions, but neither word seems to cover all that the Greek conveys. Professor F. F. Brice has observed,

This characterisation of the Athenians was not necessarily intended by Paul to be complimentary; the expressions he used may also mean 'rather superstitious'.[3]

It may well be that the Greek word covers both ideas in its range of meaning, referring to an awareness deeply ingrained in the human mind that there are powers other than physical.

This is the general attitude of the Bible. In the Old Testament it is only 'the fool' who 'says in his heart, "There is no god"'.[4] The writers of the New Testament everywhere make the same assumption, that man has some religion, no matter how distorted or debased it is. Religion then is normal for the human race, whereas lack of it is abnormal.

Some have asserted the opposite view, that it is religion that is abnormal, while lack of it is a sign of healthy normality. Freud regarded this supposed abnormality as a neurosis, which seeks to solve its problems by projecting on to an imagined God the desire for a father. It never seems to have occurred to him that his own lack of religion could be accounted for in similar terms, and arising out of the bad relationship he suffered with his father. Judging from the way that some have fastened on to the well known statement of Karl Marx that religion is an opiate to keep the under-privileged masses content with their lot, one could gather that it had been invented by capitalists, although there is evidence that Marx himself thought more deeply about religion than that.

It is, however, the Bible view that is born out by evidence. There may be many individuals who profess to be atheists, but there has never been a race of men without some belief in the supernatural, even if it has been nothing more than a primitive animism. Cicero once claimed, 'There is no nation so barbarous, no race so savage, as not to be fully persuaded of the being of God.'[5]

Perhaps it is because religion is so much part of man's nature, that years of militant atheism in Soviet Russia, with all its senseless persecutions, have failed to obliterate it from the minds of its people. The revelations of Svetlana, Stalin's daughter are significant here. Perhaps, too, this is why, if men are put under sufficient pressure, they will feel out for a God who has become their only hope. I once heard a former naval officer speaking of his wartime experiences. He told of how, after his ship had been sunk, he spent some days in an open boat with a few of his comrades. Some of them had claimed to have renounced all religion, and had often sneered at the speaker's Christian profession. Faced with the increasing likelihood of death as they gradually weakened, one of them eventually suggested that he might pray for them, and they all readily agreed. 'By the time we were rescued,' he concluded, 'there wasn't an atheist left among us.'

There is a rather unexpected and remarkable admission by Julian Huxley, avowed atheist though he is, that man functions better if he acts as though God is there. Here is Francis Schaeffer's comment:

These thinkers are saying in effect that man can only function as man for an extended period of time if he acts on the assumption that a lie (that the personal God of Christianity is there) is true. You cannot find any deeper despair than this for a sensitive person.[6]

And this was Paul's assessment of Athens. In spite of the professed atheism of many of his hearers, all around him were evidences that men recognised their need for God, and their many idols were examples of their clumsy attempts to find him. And this brings us to the second observation that Paul makes about his hearers. Not only is he surrounded by indications that man is 'incurably religious', but he has spotted one particular altar that speaks volumes — the altar 'to an unknown god'.

Other writers refer to such altars, such as an example which has been discovered at Pergamum. With its inscription, 'to unknown gods', it is comparable to the one that Paul found in Athens. We need not concern ourselves with what the original intention behind their erection might have been. Perhaps it was nothing more than to ensure that no god had been overlooked. What is of interest to us, though, is the use that Paul made of the one he had come across in Athens. As he saw it, there was irony in it, that after filling every corner of the city with altars to every deity they could think of, they were still worshipping in ignorance. This is how he put it to them:

For as I passed along, and observed the objects of your worship, I found also an altar with this inscription, 'To an unknown god'. What therefore you worship as unknown, this I proclaim to you.'[7]

The rendering 'you worship as unknown' is not altogether a happy one, as it could imply that God is unknowable. It is a Greek present participle, which literally means, 'you worship not knowing'. Professor N. B. Stonehouse points to the true significance of this when he writes:

The ignorance rather than the worship is thus underscored, and Paul is indicating that he will inform them with regard to that concerning which they acknowledge ignorance.

According to him the trouble with the RSV rendering is that it

fails to make clear that Paul is characterising the *worshippers* as without knowledge rather than the object of worship as being, from his own point of view, as such unknown.

So it was not a case that God could not be known, but rather that the Athenians had failed to find him.

This ignorance of God is even more striking when we recall the background against which Paul was speaking. He was not addressing uncivilised savages, but a community which, with some justification, took a pride in the quality of their intellectual life. Athens was an academic centre and could boast some illustrious names among its thinkers, such as Plato, Socrates and Aristotle, to name three of the best known. Yet in spite of them all Paul still made his round assertion, 'The world did not know God through wisdom.'[9]

It is natural to enquire why this should be. Why should the ancient Greeks, who numbered among them the great philosophers of the ancient world, make such poor progress in discovering the truth about God? Yet this was not the only field in which they failed to attain knowledge. Take for example chemistry. One view which was current among them was that everything comes ultimately from water. Another theory propounded by one of their philosophers was that air was the primary substance of the material world, while another philosopher came to the rival conclusion that fire was the fundamental principle. Finally there was the great Aristotle himself, who settled for four elements — earth, fire, air and water!

A recent book about science and Christianity opens its first chapter with a very pertinent question about all this:

Why did the Greeks, with all their magnificent intellectual and cultural achievements, fail to initiate and sustain the rise of science 2,000 years ago? Why did the scientific revolution begin in earnest in the sixteenth century and flourish from then onwards?[10]

And just to rub it in, the answer to this question about why the modern scientific movement was born in the sixteenth century, is mainly because, as a result of the Reformation, Christendom rejected Aristotle whose views had become orthodoxy during medieval times, in favour of a biblical way of thinking.[11]

Now why were these ancient Greek scientific theories so wide of the mark? And why were the ideas of Aristotle such a hindrance to scientific progress? They never doubted that the universe is subject to laws and is therefore capable of explanation, and yet they made little progress in discovering such an explanation. Now of the reasons Professor Malcolm Jeeves advances for this, there is one which is of particular interest to us:

> Because the mind of man was rational, the Greeks elevated the processes of intuition and the use of reason above careful observation.[12]

Jeeves then rounds off this point with a quotation from W. K. C. Guthrie: '... the philosophers tried to explain nature while shutting their eyes.'[13]

Of course it was largely Sir Francis Bacon in the seventeenth century who persuaded scientific investigators to cease from 'shutting their eyes', so that explanations about the nature of matter began to be based on the experimental method. In this way modern developments in chemistry and physics had their birth.

Now this over reliance on reason may not have hindered the ancient Greeks from being competent pure mathematicians, but it was quite inadequate as a method for discovering the

facts of physics and chemistry. And the same can be said of
their attempts to find God. He is not to be found by speculation
and philosophy, even when it is the mind of a Socrates or an
Aristotle that is engaged in it. Nor, to express the same approach at a more popular level, is he to be found by wishful
thinking. It may, for example, be a pleasant thought to imagine
that God is love, but that in itself is no guarantee that it is true.
'I like to think . . .' as some people introduce their religious
opinions, is hardly a firm basis for our convictions. Surely if we
are left to rely solely on our own wisdom and guess work none
of us can hope to be anything other than agnostic.

Paul, however, claimed to offer his audience something far
better than that when he assured his enquirers: 'What therefore
you worship as unknown, this I proclaim to you.'[14] Remember
what Paul is doing: he is explaining to the Athenians his ministry in the market place, which had as its main emphasis, 'Jesus
and the resurrection'. He might well have put it like this:
'When I argue that Jesus was more than a man, and tell you of
the evidence for his resurrection, I am showing you grounds for
believing in the existence and nature of God, whom you can
find in no other way.' We may indeed be unable to find God
through the limitations of our minds, but God has come to us in
the person of Jesus Christ and revealed himself through his
incarnate life. How do I know that God is a father, that he is
righteous and that he loves his creatures? Is it because these
ideas appeal to my reason or my feelings? That provides no
ground for our finite minds to believe anything. No, the reason
for believing these and other facts about God, is the discovery
that God himself has disclosed them in the person and life of
Christ.

Next there is the word 'proclaim' that calls for some
comment. Professor Stonehouse makes the important observation that it 'is used frequently in the Acts and Pauline
epistles of the official apostolic proclamation of the Gospel.'[15]
He can cite a number of examples from New Testament usage
to illustrate his point. 'The word of God' is 'proclaimed' by

Paul and Barnabas;[16] 'the testimony of God' was 'proclaimed' to the Corinthians;[17] the 'gospel' is 'proclaimed' by divine appointment;[18] along with many other instances which could be quoted.[19]

Coupled with word 'proclaim' is the emphatic personal pronoun 'I'. What Paul is doing here then, is not only claiming that God had revealed himself to man in 'Jesus and the resurrection', but that he, Paul, is one of God's appointed witnesses of these great events. This is a claim that he asserts with equal force elsewhere. When writing to the Corinthians he supplies them with a list of witnesses of the resurrection and includes himself:

'Last of all, as to one untimely born, he appeared also to me.'[20] This he regarded as a qualification for him to call himself an apostle: 'Am not I an apostle? Have not I seen Jesus our Lord?'[21] So Paul clearly considered himself to be included among those 'who were chosen by God as witnesses'.[22] Indeed in his letter to the Galatians he claims that the very doctrine that he taught, was given by God through a direct revelation.[23]

What then do we learn from Paul about presenting the Gospel to complete pagans? To say that he did not use the Bible could be misleading. Although, as we shall see, he gives a view of God that is strongly reminiscent of Old Testament teaching, there are no proof texts from it that assume that his hearers already accept the authority of the Old Testament. What about the New Testament, however? He certainly could not quote from it as we might today, for the obvious reason that it was not yet written. Yet at the same time there was a certain sense in which the Athenians *were* being exposed to the New Testament, in that the one who was addressing them was one of its inspired writers. And when Paul used the expression 'I proclaim' which, as we have seen, was used to denote the authoritative proclamation of an Apostle, he was really claiming the same authority as he did for his teaching in the epistles when he maintained, 'what I am writing to you is a command of the Lord.'[24]

It is with this that the unbelievers in every age must be confronted — the claims of the New Testament apostles. They may not regard their writings as inspired in the way that committed Christians do. Yet at the same time the claims of the apostles concerning Jesus, whose resurrection they insist they witnessed, cannot be brushed aside without a thought. They demand a verdict, whether in first century pagan Athens, or in the sophisticated world of the twentieth century.

8

The Personal God

If, as Paul claimed, God has answered our natural ignorance about him, by revealing himself through 'Jesus and the resurrection', our next question must surely be concerned with what God has shown himself to be like. Or to pick up another thread from our last chapter, if Paul was one of God's chosen witnesses of the historical events concerning Jesus, and therefore was able to assert with apostolic authority, 'this I proclaim to you,' what kind of God was he in fact proclaiming to them?

Those who had seen Jesus in the flesh, were expected to have learned something about God who was disclosing himself through him. This was the point of Jesus' reply to Philip in the upper room when he asked, 'Lord, show us the Father.' Jesus replied,

> Have I been with you so long, and yet you do not know me, Philip? He who has seen me has seen the Father; how can you say, 'Show us the Father?' Do you not believe that I am in the Father and the Father in me?[1]

Yet there is no suggestion in the teaching of Jesus that he was revealing God for the first time. He constantly assumed that his Father was the God of the Old Testament Scriptures, which, in common with his hearers, he regarded as the Word of God. Paul too shared this presupposition as he frequently indicated in his own writings. And it was the nature and character of God as it is set forth in the Old Testament that Paul found confirmed in the person of Christ. Paul would have assented to the opening declaration of the epistle to the Hebrews:

In many and various ways God spoke of old to our fathers by the prophets; but in these last days he has spoken to us by Son, whom he has appointed the heir of all things . . .[2]

In Athens, as we have already observed, Paul does not rely on the Old Testament for proof texts. The truth of what he says rests on the person and resurrection of Jesus. At the same time, however, it is perfectly clear that it was the God of the Old Testament that Jesus has revealed, and whom Paul was proclaiming, and Paul finds it comes naturally to express himself in Old Testament language. Look at the way he begins: 'The God who made the world and everything in it . . .'[3] This is an unmistakable allusion to Exodus 20:11, where we find language which is repeated throughout the Old Testament. The same can be said of the words which follow: the 'Lord of heaven and earth does not live in shrines made by man'. This recalls a sentence in Solomon's prayer at the dedication of the temple.[4]

What then is one of the most distinctive features of the God of the Bible? It is that he is a personal God who has a particular relationship with his creatures. In this he corrects both extremes represented by the two schools of philosophy in Athens, and which we briefly described in chapter 4. To the Epicureans God, or the gods, have no interest in creation, but leave it to the mercy of chance. For them God was unapproachable and unknowable, and so there was no prospect of any personal relationship with him. The Stoics, on the other hand, were pantheistic. That is, God was totally immanent in the world in the sense that there is nothing of him outside of it. He is its soul, so this again makes God impersonal.

The biblical revelation of God corrects both these extremes. On the one hand God is transcendant, elevated above his creation. But this is not the whole truth about him. If it were, God would be beyond man's reach and therefore unknowable by him. In the Bible, however, this truth is balanced by another equally essential. God is also immanent. So although quite dis-

tinct from the universe as a separate being, God is none the less
constantly at work in it, directing it, sustaining it and operating
its laws which he himself has established. Above all he has a
special relationship with man, who enjoys the privileged status
as the crown of creation. We find both these emphases all
through the Bible, but perhaps no statement is clearer than the
one in the prophet Isaiah which brings together these truths in
perfect balance:

> Thus says the high and lofty One who inhabits eternity,
> whose name is Holy: 'I dwell in the high and holy place, and
> also with him who is of a contrite and humble spirit.[5]

Now it is this same balance of truth which the Apostle main-
tains in his discourse to the Athenian leaders. He begins by
stressing the transcendence of God and in this he provides a
corrective to the Stoics. But he moves immediately to the close
relationship that God holds with his creation, especially with
man, and here he is articulating a truth which the Epicureans
ignored.

THE TRANSCENDENCE OF GOD

Here Paul makes four basic points. To begin with he describes
God as the creator of 'the world and everything in it'.[3] And this
creator is no intermediate being or Demiurge; he is the 'Lord of
heaven and earth'. Secondly his immensity forbids that he
should be confined within man-made shrines. We have already
noted that this recalls some words of Solomon and the dedication of the temple. Isaiah made the same point:

> Thus says the Lord, 'Heaven is my throne, and the earth is
> my footstool; what is the house which you would build for
> me, and what is the place for my rest?'[6]

It was the recognition of this same truth which led Stephen into
trouble with the Jerusalem authorities. His defence was simply

to reaffirm the inadequacy of any building, even Solomon's or Herod's Temple, to house the eternal God, and he appealed to this same statement from Isaiah.[7] But he and Paul might have said to their respective hearers, in the words of J. B. Phillips' well-known book title, 'Your God is too small'.

Paul's third point is to stress the self sufficiency of God: 'nor is he served by human hands, as though he needed anything.'[8] Men are not required to worship God because he cannot do without it, as though he were an inadequate and insecure personality who needs constant confirmation of his greatness and who hungers after admiration. Here is another distortion which the Old Testament opposed.[9] In fact it is quite the opposite as Paul asserts in his fourth point: 'since he himself gives to all men life and breath and everything'.[8] In other words far from God needing us, it is we who need him on whom our very life depends. And it is God's will that we should recognise this need and seek after him. It is with this in view that he has ordered men's affairs,[10] 'that they should seek God, in the hope that they might feel after him and find him.'[11]

It is worth mentioning the importance to the birth of science of this stress on an intelligent creator. The confusion of God with creation renders true science impossible. It may take the form of idolatry in which God is conceived of in material terms. Or it may be animism which assumes that natural effects are produced by spirits. If a chemical reaction, such as the fizzing that results from adding an acid to chalk, is simply a spirit at work, then there is no place for scientific questions to be asked. Pantheism which was popular among many of Paul's hearers, has a similar effect. Belief in the transcendence of God, however, leaves room for secondary causes to operate, which is the realm investigated by science. According to one interpretation these supernatural forces believed to be at work in the world are the 'elemental spirits' which Paul was referring to when he wrote:

When we were children, we were slaves to the elemental

spirits of the universe. But when the time had fully come, God sent forth his Son . . . so that we might receive adoption as sons.[12]

Bishop Lesslie Newbigin describes this as the New Testament's 'own account of man's coming of age'.[13]

It was of course many centuries before biblical teaching was given the opportunity to open the door to the rise of the scientific movement. When it did it is hardly surprising that a high proportion of the pioneers in science were committed Christians, sometimes ordained ministers. They were compelled by a firm belief that the world around them was operated by rational laws which had been devised by the Creator who had revealed himself in the Bible. As C. S. Lewis has remarked,

> Men became scientific because they expected Law in Nature, and they expected Law in Nature because they believed in a Legislator.[14]

Today has witnessed a decline in belief in a personal God. Modern scientific man has decided to shake off the beliefs to which he has owed so much. Is it not significant that this has been accompanied by the growth of superstition, a revival in astrology and a turning to other unscientific ideas? And this is taking place in Western countries which have stood to gain most from the progress of science. The trouble is that there are still questions which men must ask and which science can never answer. If they have lost all knowledge of a personal Creator, where else is there to turn? Bishop Newbigin concludes:

> Questions about personal destiny, about the meaning and purpose of human life, will always be asked, whatever the umpires of the language game may say. If there is no doctrine of divine providence then the vacuum will be filled by some kind of belief in luck, in fate, or in the stars.[15]

THE IMMANENCE OF GOD

Paul also had to correct the opposite error of the Epicureans, who believed that God was solely transcendent, and had left the world to be operated by chance. Early progress in science led in the eighteenth century to the same extreme, usually known as deism. The main difference was that, instead of leaving the universe to chance, it was supposed that God had left it to be operated by the laws he had established. So impressive did these laws which were being discovered appear to be, that it seemed as though once God had created the universe, he was no longer needed. The laws of nature were sufficient to maintain creation without any further divine intervention or providence. God has sometimes, according to this theory, been likened to a watch-maker, who has made a watch which, once it has been wound up, will continue to run without any further maintenance.

All this represents the other extreme which the Apostle found it necessary to correct. God has left creation neither to the mercy of chance, not to the autonomy of the laws which he has devised. Instead he is very much involved in the world and especially in the affairs of men. As Paul continues, 'Yet he is not far from each one of us.'[16]

Here again is a truth frequently stressed in Scripture. We have, for example, Psalm 139 with its extensive statement of God's presence everywhere throughout creation.[17] The prophet Jeremiah says the same:

Am I a God at hand, says the Lord, and not a God afar off? Can a man hide himself in secret places so that I cannot see him? says the Lord. Do I not fill heaven and earth? says the Lord.[18]

Although God's immanence makes possible his providential control over the entire creation, Paul refers particularly to his sustaining activity in the lives of men. He does so in the language of two Greek poets which would no doubt have been familiar to his audience:

'In him we live and move and have our being'; as even some of your poets have said, 'For we are indeed his offspring.[19]

Far from being at the mercy of chance or impersonal laws of nature, we depend upon a living and personal God for our life, activity and existence.

In speaking of the immanence of God, Paul has introduced yet another crucial theme which has far-reaching implications — the Bible view of man. And this will not surprise us, because a person's conception of God will lead inevitably to a corresponding view of man. In general it may be said, that a low or degraded view of God will involve a similar attitude to man. We can see this working out in the pagan society of Paul's day. Side by side with the views of God which we have described, was a very low value placed on human life. There was widespread cruelty, especially in the treatment of slaves, and even children were often ill-treated without question. To the superior Athenians non-Greeks were inferior. But when Paul introduced the Athenians to the personal God who had made himself known through Christ, and who is both transcendent and immanent, they also found themselves faced with a far more uplifting view of the worth of man.

This is reminiscent of a striking example in the Old Testament of an awareness of the worth of man coming in the context of these two fundamental doctrines of the relationships of God to his creation. It is in a Psalm which begins by viewing with awe and wonder the transcendent glory of God in creation. As the Psalmist passes on to recall that this same God cares providentially for men, he finds himself compelled to ask, 'what is man?'

When I look at thy heavens, the work of thy fingers, the

moon and the stars which thou hast established; what is man
that thou art mindful of him, and the son of man that thou
dost care for him?[20]

To this biblical doctrine of man, and its challenge to a pagan
society, we must now devote ourselves.

God's Offspring

One of the characteristics of our present pagan society is an increasingly secular view of man. It is a view which regards him as nothing more than a body. Even the highest experiences of his life, his emotions, thoughts, opinions, morality and appreciation of art and beauty, are to be accounted for solely in terms of electrical impulses in the brain and nervous system and chemical changes in his glands. He is, in short, a complex organic machine and no more.

We ought to be under no illusions as to what this does for our attitude to life, if we follow it through to its unavoidable logical conclusions. C. S. Lewis has described what science does for us, when it is combined with an undiluted materialism:

> Science atomises and destroys every worthwhile thing that it looks at. A loved one becomes proteins and electrical impulses. Music is just vibrations. Responsibility vanishes into causes and effects.[1]

In all fairness we ought to add that science need not lead to this state of affairs. There are many taking the lead today in various scientific fields who would strongly dissociate themselves from such a view. They would be as ready as any to study the way in which the body, including the brain, functions, and the part its processes play in the highest of our experiences. But they would stop short of claiming that this is the whole story. Science, they may put it, tries to answer the question 'how?' but is not equipped to answer the deeper question 'why?'. When, however, science is isolated from a spiritual view of man, then the accusation of C. S. Lewis sticks.

Of course people often resist the logic of their position. Church-goers are sometimes said to be guilty of this, when they fail to work out in everyday life what they profess and sing about on Sunday. We feel entitled to ask whether a materialistic scientist is guilty of the same thing, isolating the theory which he assumes in the laboratory from his social and home life. Or does he really treat his wife and children as complex arrangements of protein molecules and their emotions and feelings as nothing more than functions of their glands? Or what is as much to the point, does he expect them to treat him in the same way?

Now it is questions like this which arise when we search for a basis for morality while assuming the presuppositions of materialism. We often encounter a conflict between two approaches. Those who feel themselves to be progressives, will not shrink from making moral judgments about capitalists who exploit the underprivileged, governments which follow racialist policies and see all kinds of unworthy motives in the 'hypocrites' who stand for traditional sexual morality. It is not our purpose to take exception to these moral judgments, but to ask on what grounds a materialist can make them. Can a materialist tell me why, if I get the opportunity, I shouldn't steal his watch? After all it is only a process in my physical brain that moves my hand to pick it up when he isn't looking, and that process itself has taken place only because my mind has been predisposed that way by previous experiences. And what right have those with such views to pose as champions of humanity? Lunn and Lean have no doubt about the answer:

If man be nothing but a collection of atoms every movement of which, including the movements which are alleged to generate thought, is the product of material causes, it is as absurd to accuse a man of inhumanity for erupting cruelty, as to accuse a volcano of inhumanity for erupting lava.[2]

If human beings are no more than highly intelligent animals, what is wrong with racialism? Why shouldn't the white variety, if it finds itself head of the jungle, maintain its position there?

But we must be fair to these progressives as they do sometimes take the opposite view. This they reserve for criminals and delinquents who, they say, are the helpless victims of their background, which has conditioned their behaviour. They really cannot help it. So in their case wrongdoing is not a sin that deserves to be punished, but a sickness that needs to be pitied. Moral judgments are to be reserved only for those who stand in the way of their 'progressive' views.

Admittedly when we are dealing with deranged minds who, by reason of illness, have fallen short of the kind of humanity that God intended, here are factors which must be taken into account. And the line where responsibility for our deeds begins is not always easy to draw. The trouble is that some don't want to draw any line at all, and imagine that to succeed in explaining wrongdoing is the same thing as excusing it. One cannot resist the suspicion that this is why some find these views so attractive. They relieve a man of any need to face moral problems in his life. His sins can be explained away in psychological jargon that takes away all responsibility. It is a sophisticated version of the school boy's innocent protest, 'Please Sir, it wasn't my fault'. But it is a degraded view of anyone to deny him responsibility for his actions, and it is hardly likely to do him much good. As usual Lunn and Lean ask the right questions:

> The doctrine is put forward on compassionate grounds. But is it compassionate to tell people that they cannot help committing crime? Does this fill a weak man with hope and resolution? Or does it encourage him in the illusion that resistance to temptation is useless?[3]

Furthermore there are other ideas degrading to man which

arise in materialistic circles. Sir Julian Huxley and other bio-
logists who share the limitations of his view of man, have suggested that the human race can be improved by controlled
selective breeding, thus reducing human beings to the level of
farm animals. It is easy on this basis to appreciate that there
can be little objection to destroying unborn babies whose presence in the world would not be welcomed by whoever has
succeeded in gaining the right to make decisions in such
matters. After all they are only little biological machines. And
then what about old people who can no longer make any useful
contribution to human society? Is there any reason why they
should take up space in old people's homes and the geriatric
wards of our hospitals and waste the time of potentially useful
humans who look after them? Why preserve life anyway? It is
basically no more than a complicated molecule which we shall
one day produce in a test tube. So perhaps the deeds of the
Nazis . . .

The materialistic view of man we have been considering is
often referred to as humanism. But is this a suitable name?
Would not sub-humanism be more fitting? Lunn and Lean
have recognised the contradiction in terms by entitling the
chapter from which we have quoted, 'The inhumanity of the
humanists'.

It could be objected with some justification that the description we have given of the secular view of man, and its logical
outworking, has been far too brief to do justice to the important
issues it raises. Also our treatment has left a high proportion
of unanswered questions. Our purpose, however, is to show the
predicament in which modern man finds himself. On a secular
basis there are no answers to these questions. This is undoubtedly why an increasing number of thinking people are
coming to the conclusion that life is meaningless, and see no
alternative to utter despair. As a young agnostic once put it to
me shortly before he became a Christian, 'I have been persuaded by my friends to give up the outlook of my nominal
Christian background. But as I have pursued this to its logical

conclusion, I have succeeded in debunking every value in life, and I don't think it is worth living any more.'

Now Paul encountered something which was basically the same in Athens, especially among his Epicurean hearers. As Blaiklock describes their views:

> It was materialism thorough and absolute. The soul and mind, according to Democritus, was atomic in structure, atoms round and mobile, and infinitely subtle. Sight, hearing, taste, were the impinging of atoms on the senses, themselves material in structure.[4]

And Paul had something very positive to say to them to counter their low view of man. He maintained that the Christian revelation not only shows us some important truths about God, but also gives us an insight into the nature of man. The most important point about man concerns his special relationship to God: 'In him we live and move and have our being . . . For we are indeed his offspring.'[5]

The Greek poets whom Paul was quoting, as he himself must have fully realised, meant something very different by these words from what Paul was teaching. Their view was a mystical pantheism which had little in common with many of the points he was making. Nevertheless he found that these poets provided him with very suitable language with which to express what was in his mind. Had he been addressing a Jewish audience on this theme we need only one guess as to what he would have quoted from the Old Testament:

> Then God said, 'Let us make man in our image, after our likeness . . . So God created man in his own image, in the image of God he created him . . .'[6]

In making this statement about man's special relationship to his Creator, the biblical account of creation does not ignore that he possesses a material body, nor that he is involved with the animal world. Derek Kidner summarises this as follows:

In both the opening chapters of Genesis man is portrayed as *in* nature and *over* it, continuous with it and discontinuous. He shares the sixth day with other creatures, is made of dust as they are (2:7, 19), feeds as they feed (1:29, 30) and reproduces with a blessing similar to theirs (1:22, 28a); so he can well be studied partly through the study of them: they are half his context.[7]

So we are not surprised that in our laboratories medicine and surgery are tried out first on animals. Nor need we be upset when psychology studies the behaviour of animals and their learning process, and applies its findings to man. His higher nature possesses and works by means of an animal brain and nervous system, even though it is a highly developed one.

Yet at the same time between man and animals there is a big divide. Emil Brunner once summarised the differences like this:

The animal possesses understanding, no doubt, but no reason. It has, no doubt, the beginning of civilisation, but no culture. It probably has curiosity and knows many things, but it has no science, it probably plays, but it has no art. It knows herds, but not fellowship. It probably fears punishment, but has no conscience. It probably realises the superiority of man, but it knows nothing of the Lord of the World.[8]

As Kidner proceeds to point out, it is the distinctness of man from the animals that the Bible stresses. Man is presented as the crowning phase in God's creation. He appears last on the scene, and all God's previous creative activity leads up to his creation. Of the rest of creation God simply says 'let us make', and there follows a bare command. Before the creation of man, however, there is a pause for counsel within the Godhead. Although the word 'create' is used sparingly in the rest of the story, in the case of man it is used no less than three times.

The most striking thing that the Bible says about man, however, is that he was created 'in the image of God'. This is a considerable advance on the way in which the animals appeared who were simply brought forth 'according to their kinds'. So if a man is willing to look not only downwards upon the animal creation, but also upwards to God, it is here that he will find the relationship which distinguishes him from the rest of creation. And it is this that makes man all that he is, 'Thinker, artist, scientist, builder; above all worshipper.'[9]

How does all this affect our view of man? It surely imparts a dignity to his nature far greater than humanism can ever afford, and at the same time it gives a sanctity to his life. One of the first deductions made in the Bible from this doctrine of the image of God, concerns the sanctity with which man's life is to be regarded. Here is how it is expressed without going into all the issues raised by this statement: 'Whoever sheds the blood of man, by man shall his blood be shed; for God made man in his own image.'[10] James even saw the way in which this truth affects how we may speak to each other. We are not, he says, to 'curse men, who are made in the likeness of God'.[11] For the Apostle Paul, it is this great fact that makes man a moral being. He surely has the story of the creation of man in mind when he calls upon his readers to 'put on the new nature, created after the likeness of God in true righteousness and holiness'.[12] So without discussing all that Paul is saying here, it is enough to note that being 'after the likeness of God' (i.e. in his image) has to do with 'righteousness and holiness'. That man is a moral being, then, stems from his unique relationship with God. But it is in the parallel passage in the letter to the Colossians, that we have what is surely the greatest of all of man's privileges which arise out of his being in God's image. This is that he was intended for the knowledge of God and for relationship with him. Here he speaks of the 'new nature, which is being renewed in knowledge after the image of its creator'.[13]

How important it is for Christians, when surrounded by a non-Christian humanism that cannot but degrade man, to lay full stress on his true greatness. The danger is, that in our concern to draw attention to man's depravity as a sinner, we lose sight of the dignity that God has imparted to him. Of course we must recognise the plight of man, and the desperate condition out of which he needs Christ as his Saviour. At the same time however, God has invested him with great glory, as the Psalmist long ago recognised:

> Yet thou hast made him little less than God, and dost crown him with glory and honour.
> Thou hast given him dominion over the works of thy hands; thou hast put all things under his feet.[14]

When Paul described man then as 'God's offspring', these are the kind of thoughts that his Old Testament upbringing would have left at the back of his mind. If what Luke has recorded are just brief notes of what Paul actually said, it is not impossible that Paul might have covered the same ground that we have. In any case, Luke does give us one or two important points that Paul made, about what being God's offspring entails. He begins with an important statement about the unity of the human race as God created it:

> He made from one every nation of men to live on all the face of the earth, having determined allotted periods and the boundaries of their habitation.[15]

We are here confronted by one of the social implications of the Gospel – the Christian answer to racialism. It is a topical issue today, but it was also relevant in first century Athens, as its citizens were inveterate racialists. Everyone was divided into two racial classes — Greeks and barbarians. The Athenians had a further division — themselves and the rest of the Greeks, for they regarded themselves as the true sons of the soil, not having migrated there as had the other inhabitants of the country.

In opposition to this Paul asserted that all men come from the same origin and are of common stock,[16] and this takes from the Athenians, and anyone else for that matter, all grounds for racial superiority. We might well ask whether Paul himself had a clean bill of health on this matter. After all his Jewish compatriots were hopelessly infected with a strong racial spirit, referring as they did to 'Gentile dogs'. Paul, however had come to recognise this very clearly as one of the heresies of contemporary Judaism. When God singled out Abraham, and made promises to him and his descendants, it was not to make them into a master race. Rather it was to use them as the starting point from which to bring the blessings of the Gospel to the whole world. In contrast to the exclusiveness of the Jews Paul claimed that 'it is men of faith who are the sons of Abraham'.[17] And he proceeds to explain that this includes Gentile believers, on the basis of God's promise to Abraham, 'In you shall all the nations be blessed'.[18]

Jewish prejudice found this difficult to accept and even Jewish Christians, including Peter, had to be convinced. It was this point that brought Paul into conflict with the Jews in Jerusalem, when they arrested him because he 'brought Greeks into the temple'.[19] But Paul had good reason for treating the Gentiles with equality. As he was later to explain it to the Ephesians, in Christ the dividing wall between Jew and Gentile has been broken down. Both are reconciled to God on the same terms, that is 'through the cross'.[20] If God treats us all on the same terms, the conclusion is, as he had previously stated it,

> There is neither Jew nor Greek, there is neither slave nor free, there is neither male nor female; for you are all one in Christ Jesus.[21]

So we now have two reasons for rejecting racialism, which are brought together by Professor F. F. Bruce:

> Neither in nature nor in grace – neither in the old creation

nor in the new – is there any room for ideas of racial superiority.[22]

This doesn't mean that all racial differences are to be over-looked, or that it is a Christian aim to merge our different cultures into a world-wide sameness. Nor ought we to pretend that we are colour blind, any more than the above quotation from the letter to the Galatians means that we ignore the differences between men and women. That we are not all the same adds a richness to human life. In matters of race as well as sex we may well say, *'Vive la différence!'* Again the teaching of Scripture does not discourage a love for one's country and a concern for its wellbeing. It was perfectly reason-able for the Jews to long for their country to be freed from the occupying Roman power, just as their forbears had sung about the plight of their people centuries earlier: 'By the waters of Babylon, there we sat down and wept, when we remembered Zion.'[23]

Some have tried to distinguish between what is desirable and what is wrong in this matter, by reserving two separate words patriotism and nationalism. The value of the former has been shown by Lecky when he wrote in his *History of European Morals*:

Patriotism leads men to subordinate their wishes to the interests of the society in which they live. It extends the hor-izon of life, teaching men to dwell among the great men of the past, to derive their moral strength from the study of their heroic lives, to look forward continually, through the vistas of a distant future, to the welfare of an organisation which will continue when they have passed away.[24]

Nationalism, on the other hand, can be used to denote a very different spirit. Richard Aldington distinguished the two when he wrote: 'Patriotism is a lively sense of collective re-sponsibility. Nationalism is a silly cock crowing on its own dunghill.'[24] It is perhaps worth noticing that this was written in 1938, when there were examples in Europe which showed only too clearly what nationalism can mean. At the other extreme Paul shows what patriotism can be, in the deep concern he had for the spiritual needs of his fellow countrymen when he declared: 'Brethren, my heart's desire and prayer to God for them is that they may be saved.'[25]

Paul's next point about what is involved in being God's offspring, is that man has been given the earth to dwell in, as he continues:

> He made from one every nation of men to live on all the face of the earth, having determined allotted periods and the boundaries of their habitation.[15]

The 'allotted periods and the boundaries of their habitation' could be taken together to refer to the rise and fall of nations. So Paul is saying that God has ordered history, as is stated frequently in the Old Testament. One of the key statements is: 'When the Most High gave to the nations their inheritance, when he separated the sons of men, he fixed the bounds of the peoples . . .'[26] And if we wonder about who has the final say in the struggles for power through invasions and civil wars, the answer is in what God said to Nebuchadnezzar when he had been congratulating himself on his attainments. He told him of the chastening that was to be his lot, 'until you have learned that the Most High rules the kingdom of men, and gives it to whom he will'.[27]

There is a further point that Paul could be making here. It is possible that 'allotted periods' refers to the seasons of the year which make possible the seed time and harvest which are so vital for the provision of man's needs. It will be noticed that the tense of 'having determined' implies that the earth was arranged in this way before man appeared on the scene, so that everything was ready to provide for him. Paul had made the point to the agricultural community at Lystra, when he reminded them that God

> did not leave himself without witness, for he did good and gave you from heaven rains and fruitful seasons, satisfying yours hearts with food and gladness.[28]

This brings to mind what Winston Churchill said in his famous 'iron curtain' speech at Fulton, Missouri in 1946. Quoting Bourke Cockran he maintained,

> There is enough for all. The earth is a generous mother: she will provide in plentiful abundance food for all her children, if they will cultivate her soil in justice and peace.

Paul's world view is one that is increasingly demanded today. Narrow nationalism and unthinking patriotism will not solve the most pressing problems facing the human race such as the shortage of energy and food and the accelerating growth of the world's population. There is no master race, but 'every nation of men' has been made 'to live on all the face of the earth' under the Lord of seasons and history. It is becoming increasingly urgent that we view the human race in these terms.

Paul next explains that God had a reason for thus creating man and ordering his affairs. It was 'that they should seek God, in the hope that they might feel after him and find him, yet he is not far from each one of us'.[29] If man is God's offspring it is natural to suppose that he will be concerned to find his paternal creator. Paul affirms that God himself expects this of him, and has created and provided for him so that he may find his creator. This revealing by God of himself through nature is refered to in the opening chapter of the Roman epistle:

> Ever since the creation of the world his invisible nature, namely, his eternal power and deity, has been clearly perceived in the things that have been made.[30]

In spite of this, man has not found his creator. This is very clearly implied in the part of the Areopagus address we have now reached. The word 'feel' in verse 27 is used both in classical Greek and in the Septuagint[31] for groping in the dark. The word 'yet' is also significant, as Stonehouse observes:

> The concessive character of this statement indeed confirms the conclusion that the goal of finding God has not been attained.[32]

What is the main indication that men have failed to find the God who is 'not far from each of us'? Of this Paul is in no doubt. It is the prevalence of idolatry. He explains this in the first chapter of Romans in the verses following the one we just quoted:

> They became futile in their thinking and their senseless minds were darkened. Claiming to be wise they became fools, and changed the glory of the immortal God for images resembling mortal man or birds or animals or reptiles.[33]

The various man-made religions in the world represent the groping of men after God. Idolatry shows how they looked for him through spectacles distorted by their own sin.

Now to Paul this will just not do for man in the light of his privileged relationship with God. As he proceeds to point out to the Athenians,

> Being then God's offspring, we ought not to think that the Deity is like gold, or silver, or stone, a representation by the art and imagination of man.[34]

This applies not only to those who bow down to idols of wood and stone. As we saw in chapter two, there were those in Athens as in the present day, who have their mental images of God too, when they satisfy themselves with ideas of what they would like

God to be. As a result all they have is an 'unknown god'. But as Paul insists, for man to fail to know God whose offspring he is, is a contradiction of one of the supreme purposes of his creation. Little wonder that the life of so many is unsatisfactory while this state of affairs exists. In the time-honoured words of Augustine, 'Thou hast made us for thyself, and our hearts are restless till they find their rest in thee.'

God's Demand

So far Paul had probably been well received. He clearly knew how to address a sophisticated audience. He gave them a balanced statement of spiritual truth in well chosen language. He revealed his own understanding of his hearers by quoting from their literature. In fact his address could have passed muster as a university sermon! There were fresh ideas, it is true, but this would not have bothered the Athenians who were not averse to novelty, as we have seen. Nor would many of them have taken exception to his criticism of idolatry, as most of the more refined intellects among them felt the same.

Any favourable impression, however, that Paul may have created, must have been brought to an abrupt end by what he said next: 'The time of man's ignorance God overlooked, but now he commands all men everywhere to repent.'[1]

Sophisticated intellects who enjoy having their fancies tickled by novel ideas, don't usually take kindly to appeals to commitment. A religion that provides an interesting topic for an evening's discussion is quite acceptable, but not anything that demands a response. As for the word 'repent', that is not the kind of language for a polite society that resents being preached at.

Professor Blaiklock suggests that the reactions of the two groups of philosophers would have been somewhat different:

The Epicureans had listened impatiently throughout. They were those who scoffed. The Stoics dismissed him with more polite formality. The true Stoic, the Wise Man of their famous concept, needed no repentance, feared no Day of Judgment, looked for no resurrection or reward.[2]

Of what Blaiklock calls the 'psychology of such rejection', he has found a telling description by C. S. Lewis:

> We who defend Christianity find ourselves constantly opposed not by the irreligion of our hearers, but by their real religion. Speak about beauty, truth and goodness, or about a God who is simply the indwelling principle of these three, speak about a great spiritual force pervading all things, a common mind of which we are all parts, a pool of generalised spirituality to which we can all flow, and you will command friendly interest. But the temperature drops as soon as you mention a God who has purposes and performs particular actions, who does one thing and not another, a concrete, choosing, commanding, prohibiting God with a determinate character. People became embarrassed and angry.[3]

This was the reaction Paul encountered at Athens when his audience discovered that the God of which he was speaking makes moral demands of his creatures. Yet this ought hardly to have surprised them. If man is God's offspring, and created in his image, then we must expect God to treat him as a responsible being. So when the facts about God are made known to the Athenians, or anyone else, God expects them to act accordingly.

It is at this point in his address that Paul lets drop what some have regarded as a hint about the problem of those who have never heard the Gospel. In our present study it is natural to wonder about the standing before God of the ancient Greek philosophers, like Socrates, who possessed many commendable qualities, but lived before the coming of Christ. Paul said that 'the time of man's ignorance God overlooked (A.V. "winked at").' What are we to make of that?

What Paul says here is not an entirely isolated statement. He said something very similar at Lystra: 'In past generations he allowed all the nations to walk in their own ways.'[4] There is also what he told the Romans: 'In his divine forebearance he had passed over former sins.'[5] The full implications of these references are open to debate, and have to be understood in the light of other Bible teaching, such as what is found in Romans 1–2. What is, however, relevant to our present study is the main point that Paul is making, and of this we need be in no doubt. As F. F. Bruce has observed:

> In all these places it is implied that the coming of Christ means a fresh start. In the present place it is suggested that God has overlooked men's earlier ignorance of himself in view of the perfect revelation that has been given in the advent and work of Christ.[6]

In whatever way we may understand the attitude of God towards man's former ignorance, once Jesus has come and has been made known to men, God calls for their repentance. The problem for many that ought really to concern them is not about those who have never heard the Gospel, but those who *have* heard it, and what they intend to do about it. And if they choose to ignore it, there is no doubt about their standing before the One by whom they will finally be judged. They will be without excuse.

In the light of that final judgment Paul calls upon his hearers to repent. God always demands this of those who have heard the Gospel. It means basically a change of mind and outlook. It involves admitting that you have been wrong. More obviously we apply this to our moral failings, and no doubt there was plenty of scope for repentance in this sense in Athens. But what is being called for here goes far deeper than the external wrongs of sinful lives. It concerns our entire relationship with God and our failure to give him his rightful place in our lives.

In the case of the Gentiles of New Testament times, one of the greatest hindrances in the way of a right relationship to

God of which they needed to repent, was idolatry. This was how Paul described what the conversion of the Thessalonians entailed, when he recalled how they, 'turned from idols to serve a living and true God'.[7] Idolatry is an example of the kind of presuppositions underlying unbelief which often stand in the way of a person coming to an understanding of the Gospel. He holds on to his preconceived notions tenaciously, and ignores any ideas which do not agree with them. Or else he will somehow adapt what he hears to fit in with his assumptions. If he is to come to a knowledge of the truth a hurdle he has to get over is to face the possibility that in some of his greatly cherished opinions he might be wrong. This is often hard for some people, but it can be a barrier in the way of finding God. This is how Paul encourages the young minister, Timothy, to look for the correction of those in spiritual error: 'God may perhaps grant that they will repent and come to know the truth.'[8]

We have already seen how the idolatry of Athens distorted what Paul was saying in the minds of his hearers, when they assumed that 'Jesus and the resurrection' were two extra deities to add to their collection. The same kind of thing happened at Lystra, where they thought that Paul and Barnabas were gods. In Lystra as at Athens Paul called upon them to repent of the idolatry which was causing such confusion, when he protested at the worship they were rendering them:

Men, why are you doing this? We also are men of like nature with you, and bring you good news, that you should turn from these vain things to a living God . . .[9]

In Athens too, where Paul wanted his hearers to find the personal God revealed by Jesus, he first calls upon them to repent of their idolatry, pantheistic ideas or whatever other misconceptions stood in the way of their acceptance of the true God.

The type of language with which Paul presses this upon them is expressive. He is not engaging in a discussion with them, nor is he making an offer which they may accept or decline as they please. Rather he is issuing a command from God and the only alternative to submission is outright disobedience. This is why the word 'repent' on the lips of Old Testament prophets, John the Baptist, New Testament apostles and our Lord himself, is nearly always in the imperative. Once men have been exposed to the truths of the Gospel, they are commanded to repent. Nor are they at liberty to postpone their response to suit their own convenience, because it is '*now* he commands all men everywhere to repent'.

Here is the ultimate issue to be faced at the final judgment by those who have had the opportunity to respond to the Gospel. Those who will be eternally punished will not just be 'those who do not know God', but 'those who do not obey the Gospel of our Lord Jesus'.[10] And with the final judgment Paul concludes his Areopagus address.

The Final Judgment

Consideration of human destiny brings us to yet another realm in which Christian truth is at complete variance with the speculations of men. Admittedly for many today the idea of a coming judgment in which wrong is punished and virtue rewarded seems a likely and proper possibility, but this may well be a vestige of the Christian beliefs of previous generatons. Some, like all of Paul's hearers, except the Epicureans, have a vague expectation of immortality. Life after death often consists chiefly in being united to one's earthly loved ones, and in this is found the main source of comfort in bereavement. 'She's gone to be with father' seems the nicest way to refer to Mother's death. But for a large number of people there is no hope of anything beyond the grave, and to be 'at rest' has become nothing more than the way to describe the oblivion they expect.

A very noticeable feature of present day attitudes, as many writers have readily pointed out, is the reticence with which some people refer to death at all. Over the past fifty years it has gradually replaced sex as the forbidden topic for polite conversation. A recently bereaved person will often find himself avoided by friends and neighbours, not because of any callousness on their part, but because of a feeling of inadequacy when faced with death.

In the century of the New Testament men seemed to have been obsessed by a fear of death. The foreboding with which it was regarded is evidenced by the epitaphs on pagan tombs of those days, which stand in marked contrast to the expressions of confidence and hope on the graves of the early Christians. The Epicurean answer to this was to destroy both fears and hopes together with their denial of any existence beyond the grave. For the Stoics, on the other hand, this was another harsh reality before which to display the stiff upper lip. But no Greek thought of any kind had room for a coming judgment.

Then what about the future prospects for this world? The popular view in Paul's day was the cyclic theory, with one age following another in cycles. Each age was expected to end in destruction with a subsequent rebirth to usher in the next. Another widely-held view has been the expectation of an approaching Utopia. This has been in vogue during the past hundred years. As the twentieth century opened it was hailed as the golden age towards which man had been evolving for the whole of his history, and in which all his problems would be left behind by the march of scientific progress. Undeterred by the catastrophe of the Great War of 1914–1918, which was accounted for as a 'war to end wars', the secular optimism inherited from the previous century persisted through the laissez-faire inter-war years. Despite another World War, an unending succession of lesser wars since and a complexity of unsolved problems of world-wide dimensions, the hope lives on.

Others would admit that the evidence drives them to very different conclusions. The basic problems confronting the human race are as far as ever from solution. The spectacular advances of the past hundred years have brought other problems in their train. Einstein, for example, could see nothing but disaster ahead for the whole world. H. G. Wells, once a prophet of inevitable progress, died in utter hopelessness, indicated by the title of his last book, *Mind at the End of its Tether.*

Now for Paul the most significant future event with which men must reckon is the Day of Judgment. It is with this disturbing fact that he reached the conclusion of his address:

He has fixed a day on which he will judge the world in

righteousness by a man whom he has appointed, and of this he has given assurance to all men by raising him from the dead.[1]

It was by no means unusual for Paul to associate the coming judgment with 'a day'. The term originated in the Old Testament. The prophet Amos spoke of the 'Day of the Lord' which was to be one in which God's name and honour would be openly vindicated. No longer would ungodly men be able to oppose his will and blaspheme his name with impunity. It would be a day in which men would be judged and punished for their sins and, as Amos was at pains to point out, this would include Israel as well as the surrounding pagan tribes.

In the New Testament this term is taken over and applied to the Second Coming of Jesus. Together with the 'day of the Lord' there are variations such as 'the day of Christ', 'the day of wrath' or simply 'that day'.[2] In the meantime the world is having its own day. This is how Jesus viewed the time of his arrest: 'This is your hour, and the power of darkness.'[3] But God's day is coming, when, to use the language of Isaiah, 'The Lord alone will be exalted in that day.'[4]

Furthermore Paul declares that God 'has fixed a day'. Man's final destiny will not be a random affair thrown up by chance. Nor will it arise from the outworking of a blind impersonal force. Instead it will be determined by the intelligent plan of a personal God, who works according to a carefully arranged programme. So there are what the Bible calls 'times and seasons'[5] as the world's history moves on towards its God-appointed climax.

As in the Old Testament the day to which Paul was looking forward will be one of judgment, in which God who has exercised his providential rule over men, will intervene as Judge. He will call upon men, whom he has created as moral beings, to render account of their lives. And this judgment will be exercised 'in righteousness'. Here again we are faced with teaching that has its origin in the Old Testament. The expression itself is used in the Septuagint version of the Psalms.[6] There is a vast difference between this and the ideas that many of Paul's audience would have had about the dealings of the gods with men. Their gods and goddesses were anything but righteous in their deeds. The god of the Jews and Christians, on the other hand, had shown himself as one who always acts righteously, especially when he rules and arbitrates over the affairs of men, whether in salvation or in judgment. It shows that God is not like a benevolent grandfather who, because he has no ultimate responsibility for his grandchildren, can afford to turn a blind eye on their misdemeanours, and so gain a certain popularity with them but eventually lose their respect. Nor would we expect a human judge to behave like this and allow his feelings to affect his judgments. We can hardly expect anything less of the perfect righteousness of a holy God.

There is a great comfort to be derived from these facts about God, and from a realisation that the universe is ruled by one who is uncompromisingly righteous. It also is reassuring when we contemplate such a God judging men. Abraham when perplexed by God's policy towards the wickedness of Sodom and Gomorrah, and the prospect for the people living there, took refuge in this great truth when he exclaimed, 'Shall not the judge of all the earth do right?'[7]

Although we may not be too sure of what to make of Paul's point about God overlooking the times of ignorance, we can be quite sure that however God tackles this problem it will be perfectly just. At the same time there is a sobering thought. The position of those who, like the Athenians after the visit of Paul, are no longer in ignorance, is left in no doubt. Such are without excuse. Jesus made the same point to the people who heard him speak and saw his works:

Woe to you, Chorazin! Woe to you, Bethsaida! For if the mighty works done in you had been done in Tyre and Sidon, they would have repented long ago, sitting in sackcloth and ashes.

Taking this on its own it could appear that there was something unfair in the way that Tyre and Sidon had been treated. But having shown a knowledge of how they would have repented given sufficient opportunity, Jesus continues: 'But it shall be more tolerable in the judgment for Tyre and Sidon than for you.'[8]

Translated into modern terms this might read: It shall be more tolerable in the judgment for ignorant head-hunters who have never heard the Gospel, than for those in Western countries who have had the Bible in their own language for centuries, have had every opportunity to hear about Christ and yet prefer to ignore him for lives dominated by material pleasure. Here is a disquieting difference between pre-Christian and post-Christian paganism, between those who have had no opportunity to hear the Gospel and those who have had every opportunity.

God's dealing with man and his wrong doing can be likened to a phrase of music. Taken on their own some of the chords are discords. But like the works of God the phrase must be heard to the end when with the final chord all is resolved. At present, because of sin in the world, there are many injustices to be put right and many wrongs that cry out to be punished. The people of God have always been bothered by this, including the way that God often allows ungodly men to prosper and their wrongs to go unpunished. There are examples in the Psalms of men calling upon God to vindicate his honour by calling wrong-doers to account. And this is the very thing he has promised to do when he intervenes again to 'judge the world in righteousness'.

This judgment will be exercised by 'a man whom he has appointed'. From the reference to the resurrection that follows, it is clear that this is Jesus Christ who is the one by whom God is to judge the world. One naturally wonders whether Paul has in mind the 'one like a son of man'[9] of Daniel's vision. It was from this scripture that Jesus quoted when he was being questioned by the high priest at his trial and which led to a charge of blasphemy: 'You will see the Son of man sitting at the right hand of Power, and coming with the clouds of heaven.'[10]

There the Messiah is seen sharing God's glory and authority, and mediating his judgment. So the final judgment is both 'of God'[11] and also 'of Christ'[12] for, as Jesus claimed, God 'has given him authority to execute judgment, because he is the son of man'.[13]

There is something very striking about this reference to Jesus in judgment as 'a man'. Before the judgment seat men will be confronted by Man. In the incarnate life of Jesus, God has demonstrated what he intended human life to be, what it really means to be 'God's offspring' created in his image. Thus there will be no enforcement of some arbitrary or alien standard but only the law of true human nature. The accusation will be that of failure to be human.

How can we be ready to face that day with confidence? It is by seeking him as he has purposed we should, by repenting of our man-made ideas of him and by submitting ourselves to all that Jesus has made known of him. But how can we be sure that God will intervene again in the judgment and that we must all appear before his Son? To answer this Paul points to the resurrection: 'of this he has given assurance to all men by raising him from the dead.'

This takes us back to where Paul started — 'Jesus and the resurrection'. It was to explain the significance of this that he had been first brought before the Athenian council. Paul ends by returning to this and stating as he does elsewhere,[14] that if proof is wanted that Jesus really will come again in judgment, it will be found in the evidence of his resurrection. So the question whether the Easter story is historical fact is not of mere academic interest. If it was true, then we are bound to take seriously both the promises and the warnings of Jesus. This is the crucial nature of what Paul was speaking about in Athens, as he explained it to those who asked him, 'May we know what this new teaching is which you present?'

Conclusion

The immediate results of Paul's work in Athens were by no means large. First Luke tells us: 'Now when they heard of the resurrection of the dead, some mocked; but others said, "We will hear you again about this".'[1]

It has been suggested that it was the Epicureans who laughed at the resurrection, while the more thoughtful and polite Stoics were willing to hear Paul again. Perhaps these latter were genuine enquirers who wanted to know more about Paul's message, and maybe there were some who were willing to believe later.

Anyway we are told of a small group of Christian believers that resulted from Paul's time in Athens, and so a new church was planted there: 'But some men joined him and believed, among them Dionysius the Areopagite and a woman named Damaris and others with them.'[2] There is no reason to assume that this followed only from the Areopagus address, but they may well have been the results of Paul's entire time in Athens. Also if some of the converts were a direct result of the address, it is more than likely that Paul explained other points of the Gospel between his call to repentance and the moment when they are said to have 'believed'.

The number of Paul's converts did not exactly compare with what Peter had seen in Jerusalem on the Day of Pentecost, but as we have seen, the circumstances were very different. It was however from the small beginnings that Luke describes, that the church in Athens took root and grew. 'Dionysius the Areopagite' became the first of a line of bishops, although we know little of the church there during the first century. By the first half of the second century there seems to have been a flourishing church. One of its major contributions was in the apologists it produced. One was Athenagoras, a second century Athenian, who wrote *A Plea for the Christians* and *On the Resurrection.* He was converted through reading the Scriptures in order to discredit them, and, significantly enough in view of Paul's ministry in Athens, it was the resurrection which convinced him. Apologists like him followed very much in the steps of the Apostle in presenting the Faith meaningfully to the thinking people of their day.

Before concluding our study of Paul's time in Athens, we ought to give some consideration to the theory we referred to in the preface which, if it were true, would seriously undermine much of the value of the Areopagus address. It is the idea that Paul was adapting his views of God to the thinking of the Athenians, especially that of the Stoics, by quoting their literature. He has even been given the distinction by those who approve of this type of approach, of being associated with such twentieth century names as Bultmann, Tillich and John Robinson. Others would deprecate what they assume to have been Paul's approach and suggest that he himself later realised his mistake. They would also blame this for the smallness of the results. Evidence for this has been seen in Paul's assertion about his preaching in Corinth, whither he proceeded immediately after he left Athens:

'When I came to you, brethren, I did not come proclaiming to you the testimony of God in lofty words or wisdom. For I decided to know nothing among you except Jesus Christ and him crucified.'[3]

It has been said that Paul was contrasting his emphasis in Corinth from what he had stressed in Athens, the implication being that he was now deprecating what he now regarded as 'lofty words and wisdom' in his Areopagus address, and its lack of emphasis on 'Jesus Christ and him crucified'.

Can it honestly be asserted, however, that Paul was accommodating his teaching to the pantheistic views of the Stoics, in face of his declaration of the transcendence of God? Having set him forth as the Creator who is in no way dependent on his creatures, Paul has surely said all he need to prevent any misunderstanding that in quoting Greek writers he was associating himself with all their views. Indeed judging from the response of his hearers there is not much to suggest that they were aware that Paul was adapting his teaching to theirs. No doubt Paul could have made a strong appeal to them had he described God, to use the pantheistic language of John Robinson, as 'the ground of our being'. Indeed if he were trying to ingratiate himself with the sophisticated Athenians, and demonstrate to them how intellectually respectable and cultured a Christian preacher can be, he could hardly have made a worse blunder than to tell them that God commanded them to repent, and to base this on a warning of a final judgment.

And then just because he quotes from Greek writers is no ground for assuming that he wished to convey the impression that he shared their views; F. F. Bruce compares this with the way that preachers today often quote Tennyson's saying that 'More things are wrought by prayer than this world dreams of':

'A Christian preacher today may quote the well-known lines about prayer from Tennyson's *Morte d'Arthur* without subscribing either to the ideals of the Arthurian legend or to Tennyson's religious position.'[4]

In this book I have quoted the writings of Christopher Booker and Alvin Toffler. I hope that no one will infer from this that I wish to be associated with all their views! This is really an extension of the use made by Paul and other New Testament writers of the Greek language. This in no way commits them to the classical meanings of all the words they employ.

Then what of the suggestion that Paul himself had later misgivings about his method in Athens? To begin with, we may observe that his travelling companion, Luke, who recorded his ministry, gave not the slightest indication that he was aware of this. Nor are we entitled to infer that Paul made no mention of the death of Christ in Athens. Luke does not claim to give us an exhaustive account, but rather picks out the distinctive points of his ministry there, which seem to him to be of significance. These were that when Paul was faced with an audience who did not share the presuppositions of the Jews, he based his argument on the Person of Christ and the evidence for the resurrection. There is no reason to suppose that Paul did not also speak about the death of Christ in the market place, and from what we know of Paul, it seems much more likely that he did. As for the Areopagus address itself, as we have already pointed out, this was to explain the significance of 'Jesus and the Resurrection'. He was able to show the bearing this had on their knowledge of God, and their understanding of the nature of man. Is it not also likely that those who were convinced, and declared their willingness to obey the command to repent of their errors, were further instructed in other Gospel truths before they 'joined him and believed'?

As for Paul's account of his evangelistic methods to the Corinthians, C. K. Barrett gives the most feasible explanation:

> There is nothing in Paul's own words in I Corinthians to suggest a change of plan; rather he intends to describe his normal practice, though this normal practice was bound to appear the more striking in such a place as Corinth. He is not contrasting his evangelistic method in Corinth with that which he employed elsewhere, but with that which others employed in Corinth. (Moffatt).[5]

*   *   *

What then has Paul's evangelistic style to teach us in the twentieth century? To begin with it challenges us to face up to the pagan situation in which we find ourselves in Western countries. We in Britain often bemoan the fact that we can no longer call ourselves a Christian country. Surveys have drawn our attention to the widespread ignorance among the present generation of some of the most elementary Christian truths. We are constantly being reminded of the sub-Christian standards of behaviour which are taken for granted and regarded as the norm. We challenge one another to evangelism with the reminder that we now have a pioneer missionary situation on our own doorstep. And how do we face up to the challenge? Often by persevering with the same methods which grew up and proved effective in very different circumstances, when the Christian faith was assumed to be the official religion of most respectable people. Others have grown disillusioned and it takes a lot to stir them into some form of outreach.

What our study has shown us is that living in a pagan society is much closer to the New Testament situation than is the comfort of a Christian country in which Christian orthodoxy in creed and practice can be assumed. We have also seen that Paul exercised an evangelistic ministry in such a situation, and although it often proved slow and arduous, it led to the planting of new churches in city after city. We are not surprised that this time in Athens, one of the leading centres of pagan culture, proved to be especially hard going. Yet even here, although immediate results were small, a little church began. What we have also had to face is that the methods Paul employed are in many respects very different from what we have taken for granted today.

Now it is perfectly feasible, when facing the evangelistic needs of any district, to begin with those who still pay lip service to Christianity. By all means let us seek to bring to commitment those whose Christianity is only nominal, and work among the fringe membership of our churches inviting people to evangelistic services and meetings. The New Testament Christians began there too. We have already noted Paul's practice when arriving in a city to go first to the synagogue where he found Jews and Gentiles who shared their religion. Moreover in the very early days, when the Jerusalem church was scattered through the persecution that followed the martyrdom of Stephen, they went 'speaking the word to none except Jews'.[6] That, however, did not last long, for in the very next verse we are told that they 'spoke to the Greeks also, preaching the Lord Jesus'.[7] Many years later Paul described the strategy of the Gospel as 'to the Jew first and also to the Greek'.[8]

In these days if we restrict ourselves to evangelising those with some kind of Christian background, and employ only the methods appropriate to them, we may continue to see results for a nlmber of years. We must, though, face the prospect that if present trends continue, we may well find ourselves working in a rapidly diminishing circle. Paul had this experience too as he travelled further away from his own country, and often found that those in the synagogues, who shared his presuppositions, were a very small company. In Philippi, it seems, there were not even enough to form a synagogue. So Paul found himself devoting an increasing proportion of his time to work among the pagan Gentiles.

What lessons are we to draw from the way that Paul set about this task, which we can apply to the scene that confronts us today? If we look to Paul's time in Athens to provide us with a blueprint to guarantee success, we are clearly in for disappointment. Paul's own immediate results were limited enough. Also a detailed account of how to apply Paul's approach in the second half of the twentieth century would have to include a thorough survey of contemporary society, which is beyond the scope of the final chapter of this book.[9] Certain principles, however, do emerge, which can be conveniently grouped under the headings, the men, the methods and the message.

By men we mean those engaged in evangelism, and here we need some radical rethinking about the type of ministry an evangelist needs to exercise and what kind of specialist help the local church should expect from him. In the past his major contribution has been to address a series of evangelistic meetings for a church or group of churches lasting for a week or two. The local Christians have the responsibility of preparing for it and inviting people to come and hear the evangelist. When the mission is over, and the evangelist moves on, presumably to a similar effort elsewhere, the onus is once again on the church to follow up those who have professed conversion and to integrate them into their fellowship.

Now it is a fact of experience that for many years it has been growing increasingly difficult to persuade people to come to meetings to hear a preacher. We are not alone in this difficulty, as political meetings are also poorly attended. Even prominent personalities draw few who are not party members. Nor, judging from Paul's policy in Athens, have we any right to expect unbelievers to attend a religious service. Instead Paul went to people where they were, in the market place. Today, if people are accustomed to meet socially in their homes, this must be the place where they are to be introduced to the Gospel.

Inevitably this will affect the role of a full time itinerant evangelist. If, instead of leaving it to others to bring unbelievers to hear him preach, he is to be involved in the spade work of making the initial contact with people in their homes, one assumes that he will need longer in a district than a week or so. He will need to work alongside local Christians, perhaps drawing into groups the contacts they make. We are not told how long Paul remained in Athens, but in Corinth he spent eighteen months,[10] and in Ephesus he stayed for two years.[11]

Ought we perhaps to rely less on the work of an itinerant evangelist called in from outside, but encourage indigenous evangelists from within the ranks of the local church? Ought churches with a one-man ministry to expect him to exercise all the gifts of ministry including evangelism? Ephesians 4 makes it clear that the ascended Christ distributes the range of gifts to different people. Ought we not, then, to look within a church for those with evangelistic gifts and encourage them to use them? Whereas every Christian must be ready to witness for Christ and 'be prepared to make a defence'[12] of his faith to anyone who asks him, there should be those whose gift it is to take a lead in evangelism. Here may well be a further contribution that the visiting specialist evangelist can make, by sharing his experience with other Christians and teaching them by getting them to work alongside him.

When we consider the method of evangelism, one of the important features that the Areopagus address brings before us concerns the language we employ. Herein lies one of the major problems of those who have been Christians for some time and especially those who were brought up in the Christian Faith as children. It is the need to express Christian truths in a language intelligible to those who have not been so favoured. This is where a new convert, in spite of his lack of knowledge of many aspects of Christian teaching is often at an advantage, before he has learnt the 'language of Zion' and is still able to express himself in terms which ordinary people can understand. But we must persevere with this. Paul had been reared as a Pharisee, and had a background far removed from the Athenians. Not only had his mind and outlook been fashioned by the Old Testament, but the religious language which he had been taught was the jargon of the rabbis. Yet he had taken the trouble to master the language of the pagans in a Greek city, and so was able to ensure that the Athenians at least understood what he was driving at. Although the Areopagus address is full of Old Testament truths, the language was essentially Athenian, even including quotations from their literature to illustrate Paul's points.

Effective communication, however, is not only a matter of language. What we say must be seen to be relevant. This is not just a matter of answering the questions that people are asking, because as often as not they ask the wrong questions. What it means is seeing that they face up to their real needs and then to show how the Gospel is the perfect answer. This is precisely what Paul did when he made their idolatry the starting point for his address. And he did not simply refer to the futility of idolatry in general, which many of his hearers may well have been ready to admit, but with a stoke of genius he picked on the altar to the unknown god. The irony of it! With their vast heritage of human learning, the institutions they possessed and the celebrated names among their leading thinkers, they still had to have an altar to an unknown god! And here was where the Gospel came into its own: 'What therefore you worship as unknown, this I proclaim to you!'

Surely today is full of parallels. We are vastly more priv-eleged than were the Athenians. Instead of the speculations of their philosophers we enjoy all the advantages of modern science and discovery. We might expect the world to be a heaven on earth, but what do we see? Men and women can fill their homes with all the modern luxuries that money can buy, but those same homes can break up because they are unable to maintain a stable relationship with each other. Vast sums are spent on tranquillisers every year — hardly the sign of a healthy society! In spite of widespread education and a rapidly increas-ing knowledge, more and more people are complaining that life is meaningless and lacking any real purpose. This is the logical outcome of agnosticism which knows no god, and materialism which views man as nothing more than a highly developed bio-logical machine. And so we could go on with countless examples of where the Gospel is relevant to man's needs today.

Our language and the way we apply the message will vary according to the people we are speaking to. If the conceptual language of our hearers is the strip-cartoon, then we have to adapt ourselves accordingly. Paul showed the same flexibility. At Lystra he was faced with an uneducated and agricultural audience, and his approach was correspondingly different. As in Athens the issue was idolatry, and again Paul declares to them the living and personal God of Christian revelation. But here he singles out God's providential control of nature which would have been of particular concern to those engaged in agri-culture:

In past generations he allowed all the nations to walk in their own ways; yet he did not leave himself without witness, for he did good and gave you from heaven rains and fruitful seasons, satisfying your hearts with food and gladness.[13]

Now, although Paul's example encourages us to adapt our style to those whom we are out to reach, at the same time we must be quite clear and uncompromising in the truth we proclaim. This too is clear from Paul's labours in Athens.

Yet it is always tempting, out of a genuine desire to commend our message to unbelieving minds, to make it palatable by sacrificing or playing down any aspect of the truth that is likely to be unpopular. The New Testament churches were not lacking in those who had succumbed to this temptation. In Galatia there were the Judaizers who wanted to modify the basic and vital doctrine of Justification by faith to accommodate the prejudices of those with a Jewish background. At Colossae there were others who thought the doctrine of Christ's person could be adapted to suit the presuppositions of Greek philosophy. Paul himself had every opportunity to feel the same pressures, as he found that both the preaching of the cross and the resurrection were the objects of ridicule to sophisticated Greeks. But Paul persisted with both truths. The cross was to him the power of God,[14] while if he dropped the resurrection, what he was left with was futile.[15]

The pages of Church history are full of examples of Christians trying to bridge the gulf between biblical truth and secular thought and in the process sacrificing vital points of doctrine. J. I. Packer has sketched out some typical examples:

In the second century, Gnosticism aspired to remodel the doctrine of salvation in the light of an oriental dualism which taught that matter, as such, was evil; salvation, therefore, it was held, should be conceived as deliverance from the body and the material world. In the fourth century, Arianism aspired to remodel the Church's Christology by the light of

Greek philosophical ideas about God, which made it impossible to think of Jesus Christ as divine. In the eighteenth century, the Deists wished to remodel the doctrine of providence in the light of the then-popular view of the universe as a self-contained machine, and to make men think of God as an absentee landlord, who had left his world to run itself. The nineteenth-century Liberals tried to remodel the doctrines of human nature and grace in the light of the theory of evolution, maintaining that sin was just a transitional stage in the steady march of mankind under Christ's leadership, towards inevitable perfection.'[16]

An example we could add from the present day is the attempt to come to terms with a materialistic society that discounts the supernatural, by keeping quiet about the miracles on the biblical narratives, or, if challenged about them, by explaining them away. Indeed Cardinal Heenan has said in a broadcast that the way some exponents defend Christianity today is to see that there is nothing left to defend!

The tragedy of this line of approach is that the truths which secular minds deny, are so often the very ones that they desperately need to rediscover. One such truth is the existence of the supernatural. It is this that gives meaning and purpose to life and lifts men out of a mere animal existence. The supreme evidence for this within the realm of human experience is in the incarnate life of the Son of God. For this the miraculous element from the Virgin birth to the resurrection is essential, for it indicates that he was not a product of human history but came into it from outside.

Paul's address before the Areopagus demonstrates that he did not fall into the mistakes we have outlined. In emphasising the resurrection he must have known full well that he ran the risk of being laughed at by the Athenians. But this was just the evidence they needed to find the God who was unknown to them. And it was to convince men of the reality of the final judgment among other things, that God 'has given assurance to all men by raising him from the dead'. The transcendence that God has revealed of himself was the very point that the Stoic Pantheists needed to face up to, so Paul did not shrink from asserting that either.

They, in common with all men needed to find God as a person with whom they can enjoy a relationship, so Paul did not leave them just where they were with God as 'the ground of their being', to use Tillich's celebrated phrase. Those under the influence of the Epicureans were missing out on the complementary truth of God's immanence. They needed to be delivered from the idea of a world left to chance, and the despair to which this can lead. So Paul did not fail to stress the nearness of God and his involvement in his creation. No one, be he Stoic or Epicurean, educated or not, pagan or nominally Christian likes to be told to repent, to face up to where he has been mistaken in creed or conduct and change the direction of his life. This too Paul did not fail to do as he brought his address towards its conclusion.

*   *   *

There is, no doubt much else that Scripture can teach us about preaching the Gospel in a pagan society. It is my hope that as we wrestle with the many problems that this overwhelming task brings us, our study of Paul's time in Athens will encourage us to keep biblical principles before us. Although nearly two thousand years have passed since Paul stood on Mars Hill, men are still in a state of agnosticism with nothing more than an 'unknown god' to provide some meaning to life. Chance or fate are still the only alternatives to the personal God that men can find in Christ. Even though modern man may spurn the unsophisticated idols of ancient times, he still has his mental images of how he would like to think of God or whatever he decides to put in his place. Then what about his doctrine of man? Humanist and other views of man on offer today are poor substitutes for the dignified view that follows from the biblical understanding of man's creation.

Then the way in which Paul set about making the truth known in Athens, gives us the kind of points with which pagans can still be challenged today. They still must face the person of Christ and the evidence for the resurrection. They may not capitulate when we say, 'The Bible says . . .' but they still have to reckon with the witness the Apostles recorded in their writings, of which they were so convinced that they were prepared to submit to cruel deaths rather than deny its truth. Everyone must some day face death and whatever lies beyond, even though they live as though this present earthly life will go on for ever. And then they will discover that 'It is no unknown God but a Risen Christ with whom we have to deal.'[17]

Notes

Chapter 1

1. Acts 17: 34.
2. e.g. Acts 18: 9–10; 2 Corinthians 4: 7–12.
3. *Archbishops' Committee of Inquiry on the Evangelistic Work of the Church* (1918).
4. Acts 2: 10–11.
5. Acts 2:36.
6. Acts 2: 41.
7. Acts 2:47.
8. Acts 4: 4.
9. Acts 6: 7.
10. 2 Corinthians 5: 20.
11. F. A. Schaeffer: *Death in the City* (Inter-Varsity Press, 1969), p. 12.
12. Acts 16:13.
13. Acts 13: 46.
14. Romans 11:13.
15. Acts 22: 21.
16. e.g. Iconium — Acts 14:1.
17. Acts 14: 21.
18. Acts 16: 5.
19. Michael Green: *Evangelism in the Early Church* (Hodder and Stoughton, 1970), p. 28.
20. Romans 15: 20–21.
21. Ephesians 3: 8.
22. Corinthians 4: 1.
23. *On the Other Side — The Report of the Evangelical Alliance's Commission on Evangelism* (Scripture Union, 1968), p. 173.

Chapter 2

1. Acts 17: 16.
2. E. M. Blaiklock, *The Areopagus Address*, Rendle Short Memorial Lecture, 1964, p. 2.

3. e.g. 1 Kings 22: 43; 2 Kings 14: 4; 15: 4.
4. Ezekiel 36: 24–25.
5. Acts 14: 15
6. The best known Greek version of the Old Testament probably dating from the third century B.C.
7. 1 Thessalonians 1: 9.
8. 1 Kings 6: 29.
9. Michael Green: *Evangelism in the Early Church* (Hodder and Stoughton, 1970), p. 127.
10. Acts 17: 18. i.e. 'Healer' and 'Restoration'.
11. Jeremiah 1: 16.
12. e.g. Isaiah 2: 8; 40: 18–20; 44: 9–20.
13. Isaiah 44: 17.
14. Isaiah 44: 21.
15. Isaiah 40: 18.
16. John Eddison: *Christian Standards* (Scripture Union, 1965), p. 17.
17. Isaiah 40: 20.
18. R. W. Dale: *The Ten Commandments* (Hodder and Stoughton, 1871), p. 43.
19. Romans 1: 18–32.
20. C. K. Barrett: *The Epistle to the Romans* (A. & C. Black, 1957), p. 39.
21. *Ibid.*, p. 3.
22. Ephesians 4: 19.

Chapter 3

1. Acts 17: 17.
2. Acts 17: 1–3.
3. Acts 17: 2; 18: 4, 19; 19: 8, 9; 24: 25.
4. Acts 9: 22; 17: 3.
5. Acts 9: 29.
6. Acts 18: 28.
7. Isaiah 1: 18.
8. Romans 12: 2.
9. 2 Corinthians 10: 4–5.
10. 1 Peter 3: 15, A.V.
11. 2 Corinthians 4:4.
12. 2 Corinthians 4:6.
13. Ephesians 4: 17–18.
14. Ephesians 4: 20–21.
15. Ephesians 4: 22–24.
16. J. I. Packer: *'Fundamentalism' and the Word of God* (Inter-Varsity Fellowship, 1958), p. 135.

17. Vance Packard: *The Hidden Persuaders* (Penguin, 1960), p. 11.
18. Psalm 32: 8–9.

Chapter 4

1. Acts 17: 18.
2. Francis A. Schaeffer: *Escape from Reason* (Inter-Varsity Fellowship, 1968), p. 7.
3. Mark 7: 31–37.
4. Michael Green: *Man Alive* (Inter-Varsity Fellowship, 1967), p. 5, 10.
5. Acts 17:18.
6. We may note in passing that science too, especially when coupled with materialistic presuppositions, has its own version of these two points of view. On the one hand there is determinism, which views the material universe as a closed system, in which everything that happens is predetermined by previous events which ultimately consist in the movements of atoms and molecules. Human behaviour is just part of it, and this is caused by nothing other than electrical processes in the brain, and the chemical secretions of the glands. The idea of a person possessing any free-will is a delusion.

   Science also sees chance as the alternative ultimate arbiter of events. Democritus, the propounder of atomic theory in the ancient world, one of whose pupils, incidentally, taught Epicurus in his earlier years, maintained that all that happens is caused by the random movements of atomic particles. When these ancient atomic theories were revived in the seventeenth century, the element of chance was superseded by the idea of a clockwork universe, controlled predictably by fixed laws. More recently, however, the view that chance is the ultimate cause has been revived by Heisenberg's Principle of Indeterminacy, which sees the fortuitous movements and collisions of atomic particles as the deciding factor.
7. F. F. Bruce: *The Book of the Acts* (Marshall, Morgan and Scott, 1962), p. 351.

Chapter 5

1. Acts 17: 18.
2. Acts 9: 22.
3. Acts 17:2–3.
4. Acts 28: 23.

5. John 20: 30–31.

6. *Towards the Conversion of England* (The Press and Publications Board of the Church Assembly, 1945), p. 36.

7. 2 Corinthians 11: 4.

8. Colossians 2: 9.

9. John 6: 68.

10. Matthew 16: 16.

11. e.g Acts 2: 32; 3: 15; 5: 32; 10: 39–41.

12. Acts 13: 30–31.

13. 1 Corinthians 15: 1–9; and compare 9: 1.

14. Matthew 12: 38–40; and compare John 2: 18–22.

15. Romans 1: 4.

16. Acts 17. 31.

17. 1 Corinthians 15: 14–17.

18. Galatians 2: 20.

19. Acts 10: 40–41. Luke's use of the word 'witness' is significant. Originally it was a legal term and denoted witness to facts and events. A witness vouched for events because he had seen them. Michael Green observes that Luke 'has a strong tendency to restrict the word "witnesses" to those who had known the incarnate Jesus. This is true of all the references apart from the last three in Acts. The witnesses are the people who have lived through the events of Good Friday and Easter, and who can bear personal testimony both to their historicity and to their interpretation. It is because of this function of the witness to guarantee, so to speak, the continuity between the Jesus of history and the Christ of faith, that Paul has to refer in 13: 31 not to "us witnesses" (he was not in this sense), but to "those who are now witnesses to the people".' (*Evangelism in the Early Church*, p. 72.)

20. John 17:20.

21. R. Bultmann: *Kerygma and Myth* (S.P.C.K., 1962), p. 42.

22. Acts 26: 8.

23. Frank Morison: *Who moved the Stone?* (Faber and Faber, 1930), ch. 1.

24. Michael Green: *Runaway World* (Inter-Varsity Press, 1968), ch. 1.

25. Many will be acquainted with the widely circulated evangelistic book by J. R. W. Stott, *Basic Christianity* (I.V.P., 1958). It is noteworthy, in the light of what we have seen to be Paul's way of approach, that after an opening chapter entitled, 'The Right Approach', his next three chapters are headed:

The Claims of Christ
The Character of Christ
The Resurrection of Christ

Chapter 6

1. Acts 17: 18.
2. Acts 17: 19–20.
3. 1 Corinthians 1: 23.
4. Acts 17: 21.
5. F. F. Bruce: *The Book of Acts* (Marshall, Morgan and Scott, 1962), p. 352.
6. Christopher Booker: *The Neophiliacs* (Fontana, 1970), p. 95.
7. Kenneth Boulding, quoted by Alvin Toffler: *Future Shock* (Pan Books, 1970), p. 22.
8. *Ibid.*, p. 33.
9. 2 Timothy 3:7.
10. Acts 17: 19–20.

Chapter 7

1. Colossians 4: 6.
2. Acts 17: 22.
3. F. F. Bruce: *The Book of the Acts* (Marshall, Morgan and Scott, 1962), p. 355.
4. Psalm 53: 1.
5. Quoted by John Calvin: *The Institutes of the Christian Religion*.
6. Francis Schaeffer: *The God who is There* (Hodder and Stoughton, 1968), p. 89.
7. Acts 17: 23; and compare John 4: 22.
8. N. B. Stonehouse: *Paul before the Areopagus* (Tyndale Press, 1957), p. 19.
9. 1 Corinthians 1: 21.
10. Malcolm A. Jeeves: *The Scientific Enterprise and Christian Faith* (Tyndale Press, 1969), p. 9.
11. The influence of the Reformation and the rejection of Aristotle on the rise of modern science is clearly shown by Herbert Butterfield: *The Origins of Modern Science* (G. Bell and Sons, 1957).
12. *Ibid.*, p. 12.
13. W. K. C. Guthrie: *Greek Philosophy* (C.U.P., 1953), p. 190.
14. Acts 17: 23.
15. *Ibid.*, p. 24.
16. Acts 13: 5; 15: 36; 17: 13.
17. 1 Corinthians 2: 1.
18. 1 Corinthians 9: 14.
19. e.g. Acts 4: 2; 17: 3; 1 Corinthians 11: 26; Philippians 1: 17–18; Colossians 1: 27–28.
20. 1 Corinthians 15: 8.

21. 1 Corinthians 9: 1.
22. Acts 10: 41.
23. Galatians 1: 11–2: 10.
24. 1 Corinthians 14: 37.

Chapter 8

1. John 14: 8–10.
2. Hebrews 1: 1–2.
3. Acts 17:24.
4. 1 Kings 8: 27.
5. Isaiah 57:15.
6. Isaiah 66: 1.
7. Acts 17: 47–49.
8. Acts 17: 25.
9. e.g. Psalm 50: 9–12.
10. Acts 17: 26.
11. Acts 17: 27.
12. Galatians 4: 3–5.
13. Lesslie Newbigin: *Honest Religion for Secular Man* (S.C.M. Press, 1966), p. 32.
14. C. S. Lewis: *Miracles* (Geoffrey Bles, 1947), p. 128.
15. Lesslie Newbigin, *op. cit.*, p. 39.
16. Acts 17: 27.
17. Psalm 139: 7–12.
18. Jeremiah 23: 23–24.
19. Acts 17: 28.
20. Psalm 8: 3–4.

Chapter 9

1. I am indebted for this quotation to Robert Brow: *Religion — Origins and Ideas* (Tyndale Press, 1966), p. 76.
2. Arnold Lunn and Garth Lean: *The Cult of Softness* (Blandford Press, 1965), p. 64.
3. *Ibid.*, p. 44.
4. E. M. Blaiklock: *The Areopagus Address*, Rendle Short Memorial Lecture, 1964, p. 7.
5. Acts 17: 28.
6. Genesis 1: 26–27.
7. Derek Kidner: *Genesis* (Tyndale Press, 1967), p. 50.
8. Emil Brunner: *Our Faith*, translated by John W. Rilling (S.C.M. Press, 1949), p. 37.

9. T. M. Kitwood: *What is Human?* (Inter-Varsity Press, 1970), p. 95.
10. Genesis 9: 6.
11. James 3: 9.
12. Ephesians 4: 24.
13. Colossians 3: 10.
14. Psalm 8: 5–6.
15. Acts 17: 26.
16. This is the R.S.V. rendering which is to be preferred to the A.V. as the word 'blood' does not occur in the best manuscripts.
17. Galatians 3: 7.
18. Galatians 3: 9.
19. Acts 21: 28.
20. Ephesions 2: 16.
21. Galatians 3: 28.
22. F. F. Bruce: *The Book of the Acts* (Marshall, Morgan and Scott, 1962), p. 358.
23. Psalm 137: 1.
24. I am indebted to Lunn and Lean for these quotations. *Ibid*. p. 62–63.
25. Romans 10: 1.
26. Deuteronomy 32: 8.
27. Daniel 4: 32.
28. Acts 14: 17.
29. Acts 17: 27.
30. Romans 1: 20.
31. See chapter 2, note 6.
32. N. B. Stonehouse: *Paul before the Areopagus* (Tyndale Press, 1957), p. 27.
33. Romans 1: 21–23.
34. Acts 17: 29.

Chapter 10

1. Acts 17: 30.
2. E. M. Blaiklock: *The Areopagus Address*, Rendle Short Memorial Lecture, 1964, p. 15.
3. C. S. Lewis: *Miracles* (Geoffrey Bles, 1947), p. 99.
4. Acts 14: 16.
5. Romans 3: 25.
6. F. F. Bruce: *The Book of the Acts* (Marshall, Morgan and Scott, 1962), p. 361.
7. 1 Thessalonians 1: 9.
8. 2 Timothy 2: 25.
9. Acts 14: 15.
10. 2 Thessalonians 1: 8.

Chapter 11

1. Acts 17: 31.
2. e.g. Romans 2: 5; Philippians 1: 6, 10; 1 Thessalonians 5: 2, 4.
3. Luke 22: 53.
4. Isaiah 2: 11.
5. Acts 1: 7; 1 Thessalonians 5: 1.
6. Psalm 9: 8; 96: 13; 98: 9.
7. Genesis 18: 25.
8. Luke 10: 13–14.
9. Daniel 7: 13.
10. Mark 14: 62.
11. Romans 14: 10.
12. 2 Corinthians 5: 10.
13. John 5: 27.
14. 1 Corinthians 15: 20; 1 Thessalonians 1: 10; 4: 14.

Chapter 12

1. Acts 17: 32.
2 Acts 17: 34.
3. 1 Corinthians 2: 1–2.
4. F. F. Bruce: *The Apostolic Defence of the Gospel* (Inter-Varsity Fellowship, 1959), p. 37.
5. C. K. Barrett: *The First Epistle to the Corinthians* (Adam and Charles Black, 1968), p. 63–64.
6. Acts 11: 19.
7. Acts 11: 20.
8. Romans 1: 16.
9. The Evangelical Alliance Commission on Evangelism produced a report in 1968 on the situation in Britain, *On the Other Side*.
10. Acts 18: 11.
11. Acts 19: 10. According to 1 Corinthians 16: 9 the reason for Paul's prolonged stay was that 'a wide door for effective work has spread to me'. It was as well that Paul had no other missions booked in his diary!
12. 1 Peter 3: 15.
13. Acts 14: 16–17.
14. 1 Corinthians 1: 18.
15. 1 Corinthians 15: 17.
16. J. I. Parker: *Fundamentalism and the Word of God* (Inter-Varsity Fellowship, 1958), pp. 137–138.
17. William Barclay: *The Acts of the Apostles* (The St Andrew Press, 1953), p. 143.